The
MODERN SEARCH
for the
REAL JESUS

The
MODERN SEARCH
for the
REAL JESUS

*An Introductory Survey of the
Historical Roots of Gospels Criticism*

ROBERT B. STRIMPLE

PUBLISHING
P.O. BOX 817 • PHILLIPSBURG • NEW JERSEY 08865-0817

Printed in the United States of America

Library of Congress Cataloging-in-Publication Data
Strimple, Robert B., 1935–
    The modern search for the real Jesus : an introductory survey of the historical roots of Gospels criticism / Robert B. Strimple.
        p.   cm.
    Includes bibliographical references and indexes.
    ISBN 0-87552-455-9
    1. Bible. N.T. Gospels—Criticism, interpretation, etc.—History. I. Title.
BS2555.2.S765 1995
226'.6'09—dc20   94–41116

CONTENTS

Preface

Evangelical seminary and college students, like all Christians, usually come to the study of the Gospels with the desire to "jump right in" and get started immediately with the positive, constructive analysis of the rich revelation of the Savior given to us in the first four books of the New Testament canon. Their teachers recognize, however, that the significance of much that they will ask their students to consider in their study of the Gospels, and much that will be referred to in the most important readings they will assign, will not be understood unless their students have at least a basic acquaintance with the history of Gospels study, especially since the rise of so-called "Gospels criticism" some two hundred years ago.

The purpose of this slim volume is precisely to meet that need: to provide a concise, introductory survey of the most significant scholars and movements that have shaped the critical study of the Gospels in modern times.

For seminary or college classes, such an overview may be a helpful reading assignment as background for class discussion that is full enough to be profitable without being so time-consuming as to preclude the positive study of the inspired Scriptures that is so necessary for those preparing to minister the Word of God in the power of the Spirit to the salvation and edification of God's people.

For those serious students of the Bible who are not enrolled in a formal academic program, this volume can serve the same purpose of providing a helpful historical orientation to the contemporary study of the Gospels.

Stating the purpose of this study immediately indicates what its purpose is *not.* This brief volume cannot present a fully developed doctrine of the nature, inspiration, and authority of the Bible, and more particularly of the Gospels; nor can it offer a constructive exegetical and hermeneutical methodology harmonious with that view of the Bible as an alternative to the historical-critical methods surveyed here. Some pointers in that direction can be offered along the way, but at least a second volume would be required to accomplish that positive purpose.

My preparation of this volume is the result of my being asked to teach the historical section of the Gospels course at Westminster Theological Seminary in California. From a look at the vast literature available in this field, it might appear as though virtually every leading New Testament scholar has attempted his own review of the history of Gospels criticism—as well as several systematic theologians!—and thus that there is no need for another. Upon further examination, however, I was able to find none that met the requirement of being both reasonably brief and also theologically attuned to the Bible's own teaching regarding its truthfulness and absolute authority. Thus finding nothing satisfactory to assign as a textbook, I turned to the notes I had taken many years ago in a class taught by Ned B. Stonehouse at Westminster Seminary. There I found both the overall outline and many of the theological insights that form the backbone of this study. Most of the strengths and none of the weaknesses of this volume must be attributed to Professor Stonehouse.

Three colleagues who deserve special thanks with regard to this project are Allen Mawhinney, of Reformed Theological Seminary in Orlando; Dan McCartney, of Westminster Theological Seminary (in Philadelphia); and Dennis Johnson, of Westminster Theological Seminary in California. And in the preparation of this volume, as in every area of my life for some forty years now, the love of Alice, the precious "wife of my youth" (Mal. 2:14), has been my never-failing encouragement.

Introduction

CHRISTIANS WHO APPROACH a systematic study of the Gospels eager to receive blessing from this portion of the written Word of God often express great impatience with having to devote at least some attention to the main milestones in the two-hundred-year history of what has been called "the science of Gospels criticism." "Why should a Bible-believing Christian be concerned with Gospels *criticism* at all?" they often ask.

Well, one answer seems clear: the Christian who has no knowledge of contemporary criticism of the Gospels, or of the historical roots of that criticism, is cut off entirely, not only from the world of New Testament scholarship, but also from understanding much that appears in the popular press with regard to the gospel records. Educated laypersons who read those popular articles—for example, the long *Time* magazine cover story that accompanied a review of the controversial movie *The Last Temptation of Christ* (in the September 15, 1988, issue)—have a host of troubling questions raised in their minds and often look to their pastor or other trusted Christian leader for answers.

Over a period of six years recently, many have followed with interest the newspaper reports on the progress of the "Jesus Seminar."

1

The members of this seminar were two hundred so-called mainline New Testament scholars from throughout the United States. Groups met twice each year from 1985 to 1991 to consider carefully each of the approximately five hundred sayings attributed to Jesus in the New Testament. Their goal was to determine which of those sayings actually go back to Jesus himself and which were later "put into his mouth," so to speak, by church tradition or the gospel writers.

What seemed especially to catch the attention of many was the seminar's method of reaching its conclusions. After each saying was considered, a ballot box was passed around the table, and each participant dropped in a colored bead: red for "yes, Jesus probably said that," pink for "possibly, maybe Jesus said that," gray for "no, Jesus was unlikely to have said that," or black for "no, Jesus certainly would never have said that." The results of this seminar are now in and are being published by Polebridge Press as the Jesus Seminar Series, edited by Robert W. Funk and others. The first three volumes are *The Parables of Jesus Red Letter Edition* (1988), *The Gospel of Mark Red Letter Edition* (1991), and *Five Gospels, One Jesus* (1992) (the fifth gospel being the gnostic *Gospel of Thomas*). In each of these volumes, the sayings attributed to Jesus are printed in red, pink, gray, or black to indicate how likely (or unlikely) it is that the attribution to Jesus is really correct. The headline of the *Los Angeles Times* report (March 4, 1991) of the final seminar session read: "Seminar Rules Out 80% of Words Attributed to Jesus."

Christians read such a report in their daily newspaper and ask: "What in the world is going on here? How can such scholars have such confidence that they know so much better than the gospel writers themselves what Jesus *really* said?!" Even our brief survey in this book of the history of Gospels criticism will enable the reader to tell anyone who raises such a question what criteria for judgment those seminar members were using and why, and to suggest how valid those criteria really are.

The fact is that most contemporary biblical scholars, both Protestant and Roman Catholic,[1] simply assume that those reading their

---

[1]The openness of Roman Catholic biblical scholarship to modern historical-critical methods is usually dated from Pope Pius XII's 1943 encyclical *Divino afflante Spiritu*,

books or listening to their lectures are familiar with at least the highlights of the history of Gospels criticism. You cannot understand very well what they have to say unless you have some familiarity with the matters reviewed in these chapters.

"So what?" you might say, "I don't want to read those critical scholars anyway!" Well, they are worth reading because—although I shall grant that you will often have to chew your way through what seems to be a large amount of indigestible chaff to find it—critical biblical studies have produced much that is of great importance for enriching our interpretation of the Scriptures. Virtually all Bible students today make grateful use of the findings regarding the authentic text of the Scriptures, the languages in which they were written, and the original religious, social, and historical contexts to which they were addressed. And the critical study of the Gospels in particular has yielded some important insights into their nature and teaching. As we shall stress again in a moment, literary criticism is simply the careful engagement of the student with the actual texts under consideration. When those texts are the inspired Scriptures, such careful scrutiny is bound to yield fruitful results.

And just as it is true that without an awareness of the history of Gospels criticism we shall not be able to learn well from those who assume such an awareness, so also is it true that without such knowledge we shall not be able to speak effectively about the teaching of the Gospels *to* those who are acquainted with that history, whether professional scholars or well-educated laymen.

---

which stressed, for the first time in an official document of the Roman Catholic magisterium, the need for biblical criticism, as well as the necessity of interpreting the Bible according to its intent and purpose, and of paying heed to the literary genera of the various biblical texts.

The second turning point in official Roman Catholic acceptance of Roman Catholic biblical criticism is often thought to be the Pontifical Biblical Commission's 1964 *Instruction on the Historical Truth of the Gospels.* This document is available in Latin with an English translation in *The Catholic Biblical Quarterly* 26 (July 1964): 305–12. By contemporary Protestant standards, it may still seem quite conservative.

The third significant official document is the Second Vatican Council's *Dogmatic Constitution on Divine Revelation,* available in English in Walter M. Abbott, *The Documents of Vatican II* (London: Geoffrey Chapman, 1966). Note especially the instructive footnote 31 on p. 119.

I recall at this point the lecture delivered at the first plenary session of the 1988 convention of the Catholic Theological Society of America, held in Toronto to consider "The Sources of Theology." In characteristic Roman Catholic fashion, various "sources" were to be considered: history, experience, authoritative church teaching, world religions, natural sciences. Certainly the Bible was not accepted as the only divinely authoritative source for theology *(sola Scriptura)*. The topic of the first lecture, however, was to be the Bible as a source, thus implying perhaps a certain primacy for Scripture. Therefore, this Protestant attended that lecture with special interest.

It turned out, however, to be a rather surprising lecture. Certainly it would have seemed most amazing to any unsuspecting fundamentalist in the audience, because it consisted of a sustained attack by John P. Meier of the Catholic University of America on Latin American liberation theology—but not from the angle an evangelical Protestant or traditionalist Roman Catholic would have expected. Professor Meier cited the influential liberation theologians Jon Sobrino and Juan Luis Segundo as prime examples of how not to use the Bible as a source for theology, because of the way in which they appealed to the message and praxis of "the historical Jesus" in support of their distinctive theology. Meier's fundamental premise was that "the *real* Jesus . . . is no longer accessible to us by scholarly means,"[2] and his basic criticism of Sobrino and Segundo was that they were simplistic and naive in their use of the Gospels as "proof-texts" for their theology.

The point I want to make here, by way of illustrating the need to be knowledgeable of the assumptions and methods of the most popular forms of contemporary Gospels criticism, is that for Sobrino and Segundo to "reach" Meier (assuming that they would be willing to expend some time and effort in an attempt to influence him), they would have to show why they consider themselves on good exegetical grounds in assuming the historicity of the Jesus portrayed in the Gospels, and why his radical historical skepticism is unwarranted. The evangelical Protestant trying to reach Meier would have to do that also,

---

[2]John P. Meier, "The Bible as a Source for Theology," *The Catholic Theological Society of America: Proceedings of the Forty-third Annual Convention,* ed. George Kilcourse, 43 (1988): 6.

and then would have to go on to show exegetically that the Jesus presented in the Gospels actually accords with the Jesus of evangelical Christology rather than with the Jesus of liberation Christology.

If you are content to "live and work and have your being" in the narrow world of those who already submit fully and unquestioningly to the historicity of the Gospels, you may well find the study of Gospels criticism not worth the effort. But if you desire to carry the gospel message to the unbelieving world, including the world of those who know something about the history of the study of the Gospels during the past two hundred years, you yourself cannot be ignorant of that history.

What exactly are we talking about when we speak of "Gospels criticism"? Well, from one point of view, of course, "criticism" is something in which every Christian must engage in every area of his or her life, because in general terms *criticism* may be defined simply as "the act of making judgments, analysis, and evaluation." And this is an activity which the Scriptures themselves commend to believers— and even command of them. Just think of those New Testament texts in which the Greek verb *dokimazo* ("examine, test, prove, approve") appears:

> 1 Thessalonians 5:19–21: "Do not put out the Spirit's fire; do not treat prophecies with contempt. *Test* everything. Hold on to the good. Avoid every kind of evil."

> Romans 12:2: "Do not conform any longer to the pattern of this world, but be transformed by the renewing of your mind. Then you will be able to *test and approve* what God's will is—his good, pleasing and perfect will."

> 1 John 4:1: "Dear friends, do not believe every spirit, but *test* the spirits to see whether they are from God, because many false prophets have gone out into the world."

> Philippians 1:10: ". . . so that you may *be able to discern* what is best and may be pure and blameless until the day of Christ."

Or think of a text like 1 Corinthians 2:14–15, which speaks of the natural person not being able to understand or discern the things of the Spirit of God, but which says that the spiritual person "makes judg-

ments about all things." The Greek verb there translated "makes judgments about" is from the root *krino* (from which our English word
"critical" comes), meaning "to judge, to distinguish." If that is what it
means to be "critical," there can be no objection to such activity in
general. The Christian is to make intelligent, ethical, spiritual judgments.

And with regard to biblical criticism in particular, because the
Bible is a literary product (though one, the Christian believes, of a
unique character as "breathed out" by God[3]), a production by human
authors and therefore completely human throughout (though completely divine throughout also, since those authors "were carried along
by the Holy Spirit"[4] to write only what God willed to be written), the
Bible may also be, indeed must be, the object of proper "criticism," that
is, thorough examination and analysis—and, yes, judgments with regard to many textual, linguistic, literary, and historical questions. The
proper goal of biblical criticism is to be completely open to the biblical
text and to all it has to teach us. Such earnest study of the biblical text
is bound to have profitable results.

As our historical survey will demonstrate, however, the biblical
critic always comes to his or her criticism with certain fundamental
presuppositions. And there's the rub (as our British friends might put
it), because—and here is an important historical fact never to be
forgotten—Gospels criticism as a literary science came into being as
a child of the Enlightenment, the German *Aufklarung,* the philosophical product in the mid-eighteenth century of the earlier English deism
and French rationalism.

Immanuel Kant (who, Stephen Neill suggests, "has perhaps a
stronger claim than Descartes to be the founder and creator of modern
philosophy"[5]) defined the Enlightenment as the release of man's reasoning from all external authority. Its keynote was the principle of
human autonomy. Thus, no historical testimony (including the Bible)
may be recognized as possessing inherent authority. Van Harvey ex-

[3] 2 Tim. 3:16, literally translated.
[4] 2 Peter 1:21.
[5] Stephen Neill and Tom Wright, *The Interpretation of the New Testament 1861–
1986,* 2d ed. (Oxford: Oxford University Press, 1988), 2.

presses the principle pointedly: "The historian *confers* authority upon a witness . . . and he makes this judgment only after he has subjected the so-called witness to a rigorous cross-examination."[6]

In an essay written almost a century after Kant's death,[7] Ernst Troeltsch provided a definitive summary of the three primary principles that have guided the historical criticism spawned by the Enlightenment: (1) *The principle of methodological doubt.* All historical judgments (including those made concerning the events reported in the Bible) can only be statements of probability, which are always open to revision. They can never be regarded as absolutely true. (2) *The principle of analogy.* All historical events are, in principle (in "quality") similar. Thus, "present experience and occurrence become the criteria of probability in the past."[8] The result with regard to our judgments regarding the factuality of miracles recorded in the Bible, when "Jewish and Christian history are thus made analogous to all other history,"[9] is obvious. In our present experience, ax heads do not float, nor do five loaves and two fish suffice to feed five thousand people. (3) *The principle of correlation.* All historical phenomena exist in a chain of cause and effect, and therefore are mutually interrelated and interdependent. There is no effect without an adequate and sufficient cause.

The Kantian philosophical roots of these basic methodological principles, and how they eliminate from consideration *a priori* the truth claims of Christianity and the possibility of revelation, miracles, or any direct divine activity in human history, should be clear.

It is interesting to note in passing how 2 Peter 3 pictures the scoffers in the last days mocking the promise of Christ's return on the basis of the principle of analogy, Troeltsch's second principle, the so-called uniformitarian principle. Verse 4 reads: "They will say, 'Where

---

[6]Van Austin Harvey, *The Historian and the Believer* (New York: Macmillan, 1966), 42.

[7]Ernst Troeltsch, "Historical and Dogmatic Method in Theology (1898)," in *Religion in History*, trans. James Luther Adams and Walter F. Bense (Minneapolis: Fortress, 1991), 11–32. Edgar Krentz (see the following footnote) notes that this "essay still haunts theology" and that "the modern German discussion is still dominated by the shadow of Troeltsch" (pp. 55, 83).

[8]Edgar Krentz, *The Historical-Critical Method* (Philadelphia: Fortress, 1975), 55.

[9]Troeltsch, "Historical and Dogmatic Method," 14.

is this "coming" he promised? Ever since our fathers died, everything goes on as it has since the beginning of creation.'" Note well the apostle's response by the inspiration of the Holy Spirit. He rejects both the scoffers' premise (by affirming the fact of God's judgment in the Flood) and their conclusion, and he thereby rejects that principle of human autonomy which lies at the heart of post-Enlightenment historical criticism—the setting up of man and his present experience as the criterion of what can and cannot happen in history.

Obviously the student of the Gospels and of Gospels criticism must be concerned to study the gospel texts carefully and to refute false arguments, which do not do justice to the actual texts themselves. The student should not become so absorbed in what the critic says about particular texts, however, that he forgets those all-important fundamental presuppositions which the modern "Troeltschian" critic brings to every biblical text. This will become increasingly clear as we review what has often been called "the quest of the historical Jesus."

The history of Gospels criticism is often referred to by that phrase, the title of the English translation of Albert Schweitzer's classic treatment of Gospels study up to the first decade of the twentieth century. Indeed, that history is often outlined in terms of three primary phases: the Old Quest, the end of the quest, and the New Quest.

What are scholars seeking ("questing after") when they search for the "historical" Jesus? They are seeking the *real* Jesus of history. It is assumed that our conception of the real Jesus must be one that accords with the naturalistic, relativistic worldview summarized by Ernst Troeltsch. The Absolute cannot be an object of historical study. The Eternal cannot break through into time. To its disciples, the essential service of the Enlightenment consisted in the banishment of the supernatural from history.

Schweitzer insists that the Reformers made no attempt to return to the historical Jesus, in spite of their advances in the historico-grammatical exegesis of Scripture, because they were still committed to the orthodox Christ affirmed by the Chalcedonian Creed (two natures in one person). He explains:

> This dogma [that Christ is the God-man] had first to be shattered before men could once more go out in quest of the historical Jesus,

before they could even grasp the thought of His existence. That the historic Jesus is something different from the Jesus Christ of the doctrine of the Two Natures seems to us now self-evident.[10]

In other words—note it well—the starting point of the modern quest of the historical Jesus is the assumption that the Jesus presented in our biblical gospels is not the Jesus of history. This is the starting point, not the conclusion reached by a "neutral," objective, scientific historical investigation. This so-called historical quest is in actuality an attempt to desupernaturalize the only Jesus to whom we possess historical witnesses.

Where shall we look to discover such a nonsupernatural Jesus? In what historical sources shall we find him? Clearly such a Jesus is not to be found anywhere in the entire biblical record. As B. B. Warfield notes, in an important essay on "The Historical Christ," "It is the desupernaturalized Jesus which is the mythical Jesus, who never had any existence, the postulation of the existence of whom explains nothing and leaves the whole historical development hanging in the air."[11]

C. S. Lewis's wily demon, Screwtape, makes the same point in writing to his nephew, Wormwood:

> You will find that a good many Christian-political writers think that Christianity began going wrong, and departing from the doctrine of its Founder, at a very early stage. Now this idea must be used by us to encourage once again the conception of a "historical Jesus" to be found by clearing away later "accretions and perversions" and then to be contrasted with the whole Christian tradition. In the last generation we promoted the construction of such a "historical Jesus" on liberal and humanitarian lines; we are now putting forward a new "historical Jesus" on Marxian, catastrophic, and revolutionary lines. The advantages of these constructions, which we intend to change every thirty years or so, are manifold. In the first place they all tend to direct men's devotion to something which does not exist, for each "historical Jesus" is unhistorical. The documents say what they say and

---

[10]Albert Schweitzer, *The Quest of the Historical Jesus,* trans. W. Montgomery, 2d ed. (1911; reprint, London: Adam & Charles Black, 1945), 3–4.

[11]Benjamin Breckinridge Warfield, *The Person and Work of Christ,* ed. Samuel G. Craig (Philadelphia: Presbyterian and Reformed, 1950), 22.

cannot be added to; each new "historical Jesus" therefore has to be got out of them by suppression at one point and exaggeration at another, and by that sort of guessing (*brilliant* is the adjective we teach humans to apply to it) on which no one would risk ten shillings in ordinary life. . . . The "Historical Jesus" then . . . is always to be encouraged.[12]

Since no strand of the entire literary tradition reveals this "historical" (read "nonsupernatural") Jesus, we must somehow "get behind" the whole written record to find him.

Schweitzer is more candid than most New Testament scholars in acknowledging the role necessarily played in this activity by what Screwtape labels "brilliant guessing." Schweitzer affirms that "every ordinary method of historical investigation proves inadequate to the complexity" of this study, and therefore he concludes that "the guiding principle must ultimately rest upon historical intuition." Schweitzer speaks of the difficulty caused by the fact that there are often "yawning gaps" in the gospel accounts. He asks how those gaps are to be filled in, and he answers that they are to filled by the use of "historical imagination."[13]

Another difficulty noted by Schweitzer is that "the sources give no hint of the character of [Jesus'] self-consciousness." Here again he concludes, "For the form of the Messianic self-consciousness of Jesus we have to fall back upon conjecture."[14] We see, therefore, that it is with good reason that Warfield comments, "In the process of such criticism it is pure subjectivity which rules, and the investigator gets out as results only what he puts in as premises."[15]

Most scholars would naturally conceive of such subjectivity as something to be avoided in a scientific, historical investigation, but Schweitzer sees it quite differently. His frank suggestion is that "historical experiment must here take the place of historical research." In that experimentation, "it is not the most orderly narratives, those which

---

[12]C. S. Lewis, *The Screwtape Letters* (New York: Macmillan, 1943), 116–19.
[13]Schweitzer, *Quest of the Historical Jesus,* 6–7.
[14]Ibid., 7, 9.
[15]Warfield, *Person and Work of Christ,* 21.

weave in conscientiously every detail of the text, which have advanced the study of the subject, but precisely the eccentric ones, those that take the greatest liberties with the text."[16]

Against this background we are now ready to trace the main currents of the history of Gospels criticism.

At this point the reader may be asking, "Why is it that this study, the so-called quest of the historical Jesus, has seemed to grip the imagination of modern men and women the way it has?" The answer seems to be two-sided. On the one hand, as we have already emphasized, modern, post-Enlightenment readers of the Gospels have not been willing to accept and follow the supernatural Jesus presented there. On the other hand, however, they often have not been ready simply to reject Jesus and do without him altogether. They find the religious role claimed for Jesus by Jesus himself, and by the writers of the New Testament, uncongenial to their naturalistic mind-set, and yet they find it hard to cut off all religious relationship with Jesus. Therefore, they seek to find a new one, one compatible with their unbiblical worldview.

As Geerhardus Vos has pointed out, however, such an accommodation is impossible.

> No one who prizes the name of Christian can dismiss Jesus absolutely from his field of religious vision; there is always some category of pre-eminence or leadership under which He is classified. . . . [But if] it be once established that Jesus meant to be that specific kind of spiritual helper which by historical right we designate as "the Messiah," then how can one refuse his help in that very capacity, and force upon Him a role of religious helpfulness which He was not conscious of sustaining?[17]

---

[16]Schweitzer, *Quest of the Historical Jesus,* 9.

[17]Geerhardus Vos, *The Self-disclosure of Jesus,* ed. Johannes G. Vos (Grand Rapids: Eerdmans, 1954), 14, 16.

PART ONE:
THE OLD QUEST

1

Rationalistic Criticism

THE TERM RATIONALISM, when used in a broad, general sense, refers to any viewpoint that assigns a primary role to human reason. More specifically, however, *rationalism* refers to that philosophy which arose in seventeenth-century Europe with the writings of such thinkers as Descartes, Spinoza, and Leibnitz. According to this philosophy, reason is the source of truth, and reason—not sensory experience—is the sole criterion of truth. That which is not "rational"—that is, that which my mind cannot see as truth—may not be believed.

Out of this philosophical rationalism, deism developed, first in England and then in France, as well as in the American colonies. The very titles of the earliest deistic works indicate this movement's concern to present a rational Christianity, a religious faith not offensive to human reason: for example, *Christianity Not Mysterious,* by John Toland (1696), and *Christianity as Old as Creation, or, the Gospel as a Republication of the Religion of Nature,* by Matthew Tyndal (1730). Aiming for a natural, rational simplicity, deism set forth just three primary tenets: (1) There is one supreme God, who is to be worshiped. (2) The human soul is immortal. (3) Virtue and morality are the sum and substance of religion.

The rationalists decided that the life of Jesus could not have contained anything supernatural or unique. Indeed, they denied that the history of Jesus has any significance for religion at all. Only his teaching is of value, and even that is of only relative, not unique, value. Jesus stood for truth—but not, of course, a truth known and revealed by him alone. By definition, that which is true is that which may be known by every rational person who reasons correctly.

1. Hermann Samuel Reimarus (1694–1768)

The original (German) title of Albert Schweitzer's classic study (in English, *The Quest of the Historical Jesus*) was *Von Reimarus zu Wrede*. When Joachim Jeremias says that the date of the birth of the so-called problem of the historical Jesus "can be precisely fixed at 1778,"[1] he has in mind the publication in 1778 of the most important essay written by the same German professor with whom Schweitzer began his survey.

Hermann Samuel Reimarus was a professor of Oriental languages at Hamburg Academic Gymnasium, and during his lifetime he was, as far as the public knew, simply a rather colorless representative of deism. In 1754 he published an exposition of deism, but though it went through six editions in German and was translated into Dutch, English, and French, it was a rather bland treatise and did not contain any bitter polemic against Christianity. Indeed, it claimed to be an apology for religion, rather than an attack upon it. Reimarus warned that the materialistic outlook was on the rise, and he called on all religious persons to present a common spiritual front against it.[2]

Reimarus had written another treatise, however, which he was not bold enough to publish during his lifetime. This was discovered in the library at Wolfenbüttel after his death, and excerpts of it were published by Gotthold Lessing between 1774 and 1778 as "The Wolfenbüttel Fragments." The most important "fragment" was pub-

---

[1]Joachim Jeremias, *The Problem of the Historical Jesus* (Philadelphia: Fortress, 1972), 3.

[2]This is a call often repeated today. "Christianity must abandon its exclusiveness and join with the best of other religions against materialism and irreligion."

lished in 1778 and was entitled "Concerning the Aims of Jesus and His Disciples."[3]

In this essay, Reimarus argued that there was a fundamental difference in purpose between Jesus and Christianity. Jesus himself could be understood quite well in terms of his contemporary Jewish environment and thought world without introducing any supernatural elements. Jesus conceived of the kingdom simply in political terms. Reimarus argued that since Jesus never explained what he meant by the kingdom, he must have believed that his concept of the kingdom did not need explanation because it was the same as that of his Jewish hearers. Thus, he expected to be understood by his hearers in terms of their normal messianic expectation, which was the expectation of a political deliverer from Roman domination.[4] Jesus announced the coming of this kingdom and intimated that he himself was to be a leader in it. His ethics and his fundamental religious concepts were simply those of Judaism. No break with Judaism was contemplated.

But Jesus was an utter failure. Twice in his ministry he thought his program was about to be realized. The first time was when he sent out the Twelve on their preaching and healing mission. At that point, Jesus' optimism was so high that he could confidently announce, "I tell you the truth, you will not finish going through the cities of Israel before the Son of Man comes" (Matt. 10:23).[5] The second time when Jesus had high hopes that victory was near was when he made his triumphal entry into Jerusalem. This "playing to the crowd," and

---

[3]In Ralph S. Fraser's translation, *Reimarus: Fragments,* ed. Charles H. Talbert (Philadelphia: Fortress, 1970), this essay is entitled "Concerning the Intention of Jesus and His Teaching." Into it is incorporated another fragment, entitled "On the Resurrection Narratives," which claims that the accounts of the Resurrection in the Gospels are full of contradictions.

[4]The same basic argument was later presented by Schweitzer, as well as by dispensationalists in support of their "postponement theory"—but in both of these later positions the Jewish messianic expectation was understood to contain supernatural elements.

[5]Later we shall find Schweitzer laying great weight on the same text, along with Matt. 16:28 and 26:64. Clearly, these texts call for careful study in the positive exposition of Matthew's Gospel. Although such study falls outside the bounds of our historical survey, we will simply observe that the Evangelist himself obviously did not consider Jesus' statement recorded in 10:23 to have been a failed prophecy.

especially the ensuing violent cleansing of the temple by Jesus, provoked a bitter backlash from the religious establishment, which soon led to his arrest and crucifixion. When he entered Jerusalem, Jesus hoped to rally the people to his side. But by week's end, his ultimate sense of failure was expressed by his cry from the cross, "It is finished!"

Clearly, neither the historical career nor the central teaching of such a man can be made the foundation of a rational religion. Reimarus's purpose in writing this essay—to show that Jesus of Nazareth has no role to play in modern religious faith—would seem, therefore, to have been accomplished. However, this question still cried out for an answer: How did Christianity ever arise on such a historical foundation? Reimarus responded that the Christian religion was established by fraud on the part of Jesus' disciples.[6] The disciples were not prepared to accept failure. They had been counting on success. They had come to enjoy the prominence, financial security, and ease of their life with Jesus, and they wanted to perpetuate such a life. Preaching was certainly an easier vocation than fishing or any other job they had known! After some fast thinking, their message was radically readjusted. They hit upon the idea of preaching that Jesus had been resurrected. They stole his body from the grave and waited fifty days to proclaim his resurrection, so that if the body should be found, it would be unrecognizable. Then they introduced the idea of a second coming of the resurrected Messiah and reinterpreted the purpose of the Messiah's first coming in spiritual and ethical terms. All the doctrines of the Christian faith were invented by Jesus' disciples and other power-hungry theologians who followed them.

Schweitzer offers the curious opinion that "hate as well as love can write a Life of Jesus, and the greatest of them are written with hate: that of Reimarus . . . and that of . . . Strauss."[7] As we have already indicated, however, Reimarus thought that by discrediting Christian-

---

[6]Reimarus also suggested that Jesus himself had been involved in fraud at certain points in his ministry. Jesus and his disciples together had staged certain "miracles," such as the raising of Lazarus, in order to "prove" that Jesus was indeed the Messiah.

[7]Albert Schweitzer, *The Quest of the Historical Jesus,* trans. W. Montgomery, 2d ed. (1911; reprint, London: Adam & Charles Black, 1945), 4.

ity—the leading supernatural religion of revelation—he achieved the positive purpose of commending a natural religion of reason.

As we have noted, Reimarus is credited with initiating the modern search for the historical Jesus, the "real" Jesus behind the gospel accounts. His lasting significance is that he raised certain questions that have remained in the forefront of Gospels criticism: (1) What was Jesus' own view (often referred to as his "consciousness") of his messiahship? (2) How significant was the eschatological perspective (that is, his emphasis on the coming of God's kingdom and his role in it) in Jesus' own thought? (3) What is the relationship between the Jesus of history and the Christ of the church's faith? Or, to put it another way, who was the real founder of Christianity, Jesus or the apostles?

Reimarus's own explanation of the origin of Christianity, however, is a museum piece today, with no defenders. Harvey McArthur points out what he regards as "the most obvious absurdity" in Reimarus's reconstruction of the beginnings of Christianity:

> If the apostles deliberately and consciously transformed the message of Jesus into something totally other than that which it had been originally, how does it happen that the same group of apostles, and those associated with them, perpetuated an untransformed version of the ministry of Jesus, that is to say, the version which has come down to us in the Gospels? . . . [I]f the transformation was the result of a conscious and planned deception why did those same deceivers refute themselves by perpetuating the untransformed tradition alongside of the transformed?[8]

Equally absurd is Reimarus's explanation of the resurrection message that gave birth to the church. It is inconceivable that the very apostles who allegedly faked Jesus' resurrection and cynically proclaimed it as true would later gladly lay down their lives for what they knew to be a monstrous lie. This is the key point to which orthodox Christian apologists like B. B. Warfield return again and again: if the real Jesus cannot have been the Jesus of the gospel records, we are left with no reasonable explanation for the origin of the Christian church.[9]

---

[8]Harvey K. McArthur, *The Quest Through the Centuries* (Philadelphia: Fortress, 1966), 106.

[9]See footnote 11 on p. 9, above.

2. H. E. G. Paulus (1761–1851)

The second German professor whom we shall briefly consider is often cited as the most typical representative of the thoroughgoing rationalist approach to Christianity that was so popular at the end of the eighteenth century, even though he taught and wrote for the most part after that popularity had reached its peak and was waning. A keen student of Spinoza and Kant, Heinrich Eberhard Gottlob Paulus was professor of theology at Heidelberg for the last forty years of his life.

The most helpful way to summarize his views may be to contrast them with those of Reimarus:[10]

1. *With regard to the purpose of his writings.*[11] Like Kant, Paulus saw himself as a friend and apologist for Christianity. The preface to his *Life of Jesus* was a vigorous polemic against orthodox Christianity, particularly against the doctrines of imputation and substitutionary atonement. He affirmed, however, that he gladly believed all that is worthy of belief. Modern people reject the Bible, he said, because they do not understand it; and they do not understand it because they fail to understand the environment in which the Bible was written. When the Bible and its environment are explained to them (as he set out in his books to do), they will believe it.

Paulus, however, wanted to distinguish not only between true Christianity and orthodox Christianity, but also between true Christianity and Reimarus's radically reconstructed history of Christianity. Reimarus had separated Jesus from Christianity. Paulus's purpose, expressed positively, was to show the continuity between Jesus and

---

[10]Critical expositions of Paulus's views can be found in Schweitzer, *Quest of the Historical Jesus,* 48–57, and in Theodore Christlieb, *Modern Doubt and Christian Belief* (New York: Scribner, Armstrong & Co., 1875), 345–53.

[11]Most importantly, *Philologisch-kritischer und historischer Commentar über die drey ersten Evangelien* [Philological-critical and historical commentary on the first three gospels], 2d ed. (Lübeck: J. F. Bohn, 1804–5); *Philologisch-kritischer und historischer Commentar über das Evangelium des Johannes* [Philological-critical and historical commentary on the Gospel of John] (Leipzig: J. A. Barth, 1812); and *Das Leben Jesu als Grundlage einer reinen Geschichte des Urchristentums* [The life of Jesus as the basis of a purely historical account of early Christianity] (Heidelberg: C. F. Winter, 1828).

Christianity as the rational religion. This he did by emphasizing the ethical personality of Jesus. As we shall note in a moment, Paulus wanted to play down the significance of miracles. In a characteristic statement he wrote, "The truly miraculous thing about Jesus is Himself, the purity and serene holiness of His character, which is, notwithstanding, genuinely human, and adapted to the imitation and emulation of mankind."[12]

2. *With regard to Jesus' view of his messiahship.* Paulus emphasized that Jesus' great purpose was to bring about changes in the moral character of his hearers and thus to bring in the rule of God for many. This, he insisted, is the essence of Christianity. Paulus rejected altogether Reimarus's notion that Jesus held to the concept of a political Messiah, but his own explanation of Jesus' messianic consciousness was exceedingly vague. Jesus, Paulus said, appropriated to himself everything in the Jewish messianic ideal that was worthy of God and fulfilled all that in his holy religion of love as the spiritual Son of God. Jesus was even willing to die as the Messiah in order to win a higher messiahship as the Son of Man.

3. *With regard to the miracles of Jesus.* It is for his rational "explanations" of the miracles recorded in the Gospels that Paulus is best known by later generations. He is usually cited as a horrible example of a position that soon came to be viewed as rather silly. At this point Paulus can be viewed as providing a bit of "comic relief" in the history of Gospels criticism!

Reimarus had explained the miracle stories as either staged events or pure fables, the kind of tale that can be expected in the development of the tradition about any hero, based often on Old Testament expectations and calculated to confirm belief in Jesus' messiahship. For Paulus, however, an understanding of the environment in which the Gospels were written is crucial. This was a prescientific, miracle-believing age. Owing to an ignorance of secondary causes and to inaccurate observation, events that had perfectly rational explanations were attributed to the direct agency of God. Something really *hap-*

---

[12]Quoted by Schweitzer, *Quest of the Historical Jesus,* 51.

pened in each case. Paulus did not deny that. But it was not accurately observed or described.

For example, Paulus explained that the healing miracles were due to Jesus' superior appreciation of the power of suggestion, his psychological impact upon the nervous system of long-time sufferers, or his use of medicines whose healing powers were known to him alone.

But what about the so-called nature miracles? Here especially is where later readers have found Paulus's explanations more amusing than convincing. For example, in the feeding of the five thousand, Jesus' generous example in sharing what food he had with others influenced various rich persons present to share what they had also. When Jesus was seen walking on the water, he was actually walking along the shore in a mist that covered his feet from view. The transfiguration scene was the impression made on the drowsy disciples by Jesus' standing on a hill talking to two strangers with the sun rising behind them. The raising of the dead—including Lazarus (remember Reimarus's explanation in footnote 6 on p. 18, above)—was actually a deliverance from premature burial, because those who were raised were not dead but in a coma. In Judaea at that time, burial took place only three hours after death, and sometimes, therefore, those buried were not actually dead.

What Paulus wanted to stress, however, in good Kantian fashion, was that miracles are of absolutely no importance for religious faith. The most puzzling event in the phenomenal world can neither prove nor disprove any spiritual truth, because how can we know for sure what has brought that event about?

There is, of course, a significant philosophy of history and of revelation involved in that statement. For Paulus, a "miracle"—like any other historical event—would be merely a brute, isolated, unexplained fact. In the biblical philosophy of history, a miracle is not an isolated event; rather, it takes place in the context of redemptive history and is accompanied by divine verbal revelation that gives us authoritative interpretation of its meaning. In Paulus, the rationalist, we see how the denial of the Bible's own view of *word* revelation ultimately leads to the denial of the meaningful possibility of *act* revelation.

4. *With regard to the moral problem at the very origin of the church.* Paulus was anxious to clear the disciples of Reimarus's charge of

fraud, pointing out that the disciples were children of their age and could not be blamed for being poor observers. However, as Schweitzer argues, Paulus actually shifted the moral blame to Jesus himself, since he presented Jesus as taking advantage of the evil of premature burial without teaching his disciples that it was evil and seeking to bring an end to it.[13]

5. *With regard to the resurrection of Jesus and the origin of the Christian church.* Reimarus had claimed that the disciples' proclamation of the Resurrection was fraudulent. No, said Paulus. The disciples actually saw Jesus alive after the Crucifixion! They saw the nail prints in his hands. Again, what had taken place was premature burial.

Paulus's view is often referred to as the "trance" or "swoon" theory of the Resurrection. This theory was widely held by the rationalists of the time. Crucifixion was a very slow death, and Jesus did not actually die on the cross. Several details in the gospel records, so it was claimed, point to factors that caused Jesus to revive in the grave: the coolness of the tomb; the aromatic ointments applied to his body; the spear-thrust into his side, which was only a superficial wound and actually served the therapeutic purpose of a phlebotomy (a bloodletting); the loud cry that Jesus uttered immediately before lapsing into unconsciousness, which shows that his strength was not exhausted; and then, most important of all, the earthquake, which served both to revive Jesus and to roll the stone away from the tomb's entrance.

After some forty days, Jesus did die. First, however, he assembled his disciples; a cloud came between him and them; and the two secret followers of Jesus who had been talking with him at the Transfiguration exhorted the disciples not to dawdle, but to be up and doing.[14]

---

[13]Schweitzer, *Quest of the Historical Jesus,* 53.

[14]Another value of an historical study such as this, one that I did not mention in the Introduction, is that it enables us to recognize that many allegedly new theories regarding the historical Jesus are not new at all. A good example is the book by the Jewish critic of Christianity, Hugh J. Schonfield, entitled *The Passover Plot* (New York: Random House, 1965). That best-seller stirred up the kind of controversy and headline coverage in the media that might be compared with the fuss in 1988 over the movie *The Last Temptation of Christ.* Actually, however, the "new" view presented by Schonfield essentially combined the trance theory of Paulus with the fraud theory of

Schweitzer comments that Paulus saved his own sincerity only at the expense of the sincerity of the disciples, whom he depicts as utterly ridiculous, and of Jesus, who does not protest against their ridiculous interpretations of what was happening.[15]

Paulus's historical significance may be summarized very briefly. In several ways, Paulus, along with Kant and Schleiermacher, was an important precursor of the later Ritschlian liberalism: (1) in his emphasis on the exemplary ethical personality and teaching of Jesus as the essence of the Christian religion, (2) in his minimizing of the eschatological element in Jesus' messianic consciousness, and (3) in his playing down of the theological significance of miracles.

Surely, however, the rationalistic explanations that Paulus offered for the apparently supernatural elements in the Gospels are most unimpressive. They merely show us what desperate measures some have been willing to take in order to maintain the essential historicity of the gospel accounts while rejecting anything that points beyond the "natural" realm of present experience. And thus they help us to understand why many later critics became more radical in surrendering both the rationalistic explanations and the historicity of the Gospels.[16]

Reimarus (although neither of their names appears in the index), with the fraud placed at the feet of Jesus himself, who plotted with Joseph of Arimathea, Judas Iscariot, and others (not including Jesus' immediate disciples) both his apparent death and his rescue from the tomb and temporary recovery.

[15]Schweitzer, *Quest of the Historical Jesus,* 57.

[16]Frequently in this historical survey, the classifications "liberal" and "radical" are used to indicate two general schools of Gospels criticism. What ideas are to be associated with each school will become clearer as we proceed—for example, with regard to the historical reliability of the Gospels and the relative importance of Jesus and the church (the believing community) as the creative force in the origin of Christianity. Since these labels are merely generalizations (though helpful ones, I believe, in allowing us to see "the big picture" in the history of Gospels criticism), we shall find that certain critics display particular features of both traditions. Here we might note that while Paulus, as indicated above, was clearly a precursor of the liberal school, Reimarus in important ways pointed in the radical direction.

2

Hegelian Reconstructions

IN RATIONALISM, reason is the criterion by which reality is to be judged. Hegelianism goes further. In Hegelianism, reason is viewed not merely as the arbiter of what is real, but also as reality itself. All history is seen to be the coming to full expression of the World Mind, or World Spirit *(Weltgeist).*

Georg Wilhelm Friedrich Hegel (1770–1831) took as his philosophical task the overcoming of the fundamental dualism of Immanuel Kant, who had divided reality into the noumenal and the phenomenal. Hegel's philosophy "seeks to overcome through rational reflection the alienating consequences of all allegedly unresolved duality." In Hegel's thought, "all oppositions are known as ultimately reconciled self-differentiations" of the *Weltgeist.*[1]

The *Weltgeist* is the All. Some may call this *Weltgeist* "God," but it is not a transcendent Creator; it is rather the world process itself. If the *Weltgeist* is referred to as "God," Hegel's philosophy may be termed a form of pantheism. Certainly it is an ontological monism (all being is the same in kind), sometimes referred to as a spiritualist

---

[1]Patrick Masterson, *Atheism and Alienation* (Notre Dame, Ind.: University of Notre Dame Press, 1971), 41.

monism to distinguish it from the materialist monism of Hegel's disciples, Marx and Engels.[2]

According to Hegel, the *Weltgeist* is the world *process*. It is for this reason that his monism is called a *dynamic* monism. History is seen to be the progressive self-realization of the *Geist* (Spirit or Mind)—not simply its self-revelation, but its self-realization. History is "God-in-the-making." All history is the coming to full expression of the World Mind.[3]

This historical process moves in dialectical, creative conflict to its ultimate end. Every dominant historical movement (thesis) produces inevitably a countermovement (antithesis) with which it contends until both come together in a higher unity (synthesis), which becomes at that point the thesis that brings forth its own antithesis that must yield a new synthesis, and so on.[4]

The *Geist* posits the world as Otherness, thus alienating itself

---

[2]We recognize immediately the atheistic character of materialist monisms (Marxism, for example), but we should see that all so-called spiritualist monisms are likewise atheistic. Pantheism, which involves a fundamental denial of the Creator-creature distinction, must be considered only semantically different from atheism. How is saying that God alone exists different from saying that the material world alone exists? As Cornelio Fabro notes, "To say that everything is matter or that everything is spirit is to say nothing at all, because with the evaporation of all distinctions there vanishes likewise all possibility of any meaningful contraposition" (*God in Exile*, trans. and ed. Arthur Gibson [Westminster, Md.: Newman, 1968], 17).

Fabro begins his study of modern atheism with a chapter entitled "In the Beginning Was Hegel." Hegel's philosophy was the doorway to atheism for Feuerbach, Strauss, Engels, Marx, and Nietzsche. But so adept was Hegel at pulling the wool over people's eyes, and so lacking in understanding of true Christian faith were the orthodox academic authorities of Hegel's day, that Hegel was awarded a medal by the University of Berlin bearing the inscription "Defender of Christianity"! Karl Marx and Bruno Bauer (whom we shall look at later in this chapter) were more accurate in saying that the inscription ought to have read, "Hegel: Atheist and Antichrist." See Bruno Bauer, *The Trumpet of the Last Judgement Against Hegel the Atheist and Antichrist*, trans. Lawrence Stepelevich (Lewiston, N.Y.: Edwin Mellen, 1989).

[3]In our time we have seen something of a revival of Hegelian thinking in such popular ideologies as New Age religion, Process Theology, and Liberation Theology: God is the future, the one who is coming.

[4]This process was not conceived of by Hegel as eternally open-ended, however, any more than it was later by Marx. According to Hegel, the dialectical process reached

from itself. Then, by a progressive coming to self-consciousness in man, it achieves reconciliation by recognizing this Otherness as one with the self. All is *Geist,* but it is uniquely in the mind of man that *Geist* comes to self-consciousness as *Geist.*

In this historic process, which is the coming to self-realization of the World Mind, there is absolutely no room for the supernatural, for mystery. In Hegel's famous dictum, "The real is the rational and the rational is the real."

1. David Friedrich Strauss (1808–74)

The first Hegelian we shall consider is a person whom many have called the most important figure in the history of Gospels criticism—although many others, such as Wrede, Kähler, and Bultmann, have also been crucial in their influence, as we shall see. Strauss was a pivotal figure because of his effective criticism of the Gospels study that had preceded him and because of the conceptual framework he provided for so much of what has followed him. Perhaps no other single work that we shall mention in our survey has had more significance than Strauss's *The Life of Jesus Critically Examined,* which was published in 1835 when the author was just twenty-seven years old.[5]

It was Strauss who introduced the notion of myth into Gospels criticism, and therefore the views presented in his *Life of Jesus* have a note of modernity about them still. In some ways he may be thought of as being ahead of his time.

Strauss began his study of the Gospels as a student under F. C. Baur, first at the seminary at Maulbronn and later at Tübingen. His academic career peaked quite early—and faded just as suddenly—whereas Baur came to have his main influence later in his life and after

---

an apex, a final stage, in Hegelian philosophy itself, which marked the end of history! As Robert C. Tucker puts it, "God had come to himself completely in the philosophical person of Hegel" (*Philosophy and Myth in Karl Marx* [Cambridge: Cambridge University Press, 1961], 43).

[5]"This year and this book marked, as few others have done, a turning-point in the history of the Christian faith" (Stephen Neill and Tom Wright, *The Interpretation of the New Testament 1861–1986* [Oxford: Oxford University Press, 1988], 14).

Strauss's heyday. For that reason the teacher appears in this chapter later than the student.

In 1831, at the age of twenty-three, Strauss went to Berlin chiefly to hear Hegel lecture. He got to hear only two lectures before Hegel's death, but those lectures revolutionized his thinking. He returned to the seminary at Tübingen to serve as a private tutor and began to write his *Life of Jesus.* The publication of the first volume of the first edition in 1835 made a sensational impact, and immediately Strauss lost his position at Tübingen. (Perhaps he should have followed Reimarus's example and published his radical views only posthumously!) He moved to Stuttgart, where he continued to write, but led a very private and unhappy life. In the third edition (1838), Strauss yielded somewhat to the criticism that his work had received and presented a more "positive" interpretation. But in the fourth edition (1840), he restored the original work completely.[6] It is this fourth edition that was translated into English in 1846 by George Eliot (Marian Evans),[7] who had earlier translated Ludwig Feuerbach's *The Essence of Christianity,* a book that had an important influence on Karl Marx and Friedrich Engels.[8]

Strauss considered his approach to the Gospels to be the true solution (and thus the true synthesis) to the unresolved problems of both the orthodox and the rationalist students of the Gospels in his day. Orthodox Christians continued to hold that the Gospels were reliable historical accounts and that the miracles they recorded actually hap-

---

[6]In 1864 Strauss published *A Life of Jesus for the German People,* in which, most surprisingly, an evolutionary philosophy replaced his earlier Hegelian dialectic (Darwin's *The Origin of Species* had appeared in 1859), and a more liberal view of Jesus replaced his earlier radical view. (See again footnote 16 on p. 24, regarding the force of those two adjectives, "liberal" and "radical.") Although a later book, it was not an important one. When writers speak of Strauss's *Life of Jesus,* they are referring to his earlier work.

[7]David Friedrich Strauss, *The Life of Jesus Critically Examined,* trans. George Eliot (Philadelphia: Fortress, 1972; London: SCM, 1973).

[8]Some time ago, I was startled to hear Alastair Cooke, in introducing a PBS "Masterpiece Theater" television adaptation of George Eliot's novel, *Silas Marner,* comment that the writer had never completely abandoned the Christian faith of her childhood, as evidenced by her later translating a work by a German scholar on *The Essence of Christianity.* Evidently the erudite Mr. Cooke was not aware that Ludwig Feuerbach's book was actually a scathing, atheistic attack on the Christian faith!

pened. This, Strauss insisted, was impossible. The rationalist Christians (like Paulus) agreed with the orthodox that the Gospels were, basically at least, reliable historical accounts, but the rationalists taught that the miracles were historical occurrences inadequately observed and improperly interpreted.

Friedrich Schleiermacher (1768–1834) was also lecturing at the University of Berlin (as professor of religion) during Strauss's studies there. Schleiermacher had put forward what he considered to be the proper compromise, a mediating position between the thesis of orthodoxy and the antithesis of rationalism, by presenting a Christian supernaturalism supported by the insights of the Enlightenment.[9] As Strauss saw it, Schleiermacher's synthesis was a methodologically confused pseudosynthesis that attempted to have it both ways. Defining religion simply as a feeling of dependence upon the Absolute, Schleiermacher is often hailed as the father of Protestant liberalism, and thus a most important figure in the history of theology, but he displayed a fuzzy, equivocal attitude toward the gospel miracles that was completely repugnant to the radical Strauss. Schweitzer wrote regarding Schleiermacher that "no one else has shown the same skill in concealing how much in the way of miracle he ultimately retains and how much he rejects. His solution is . . . an attempt to transcend the necessity for a rationalistic explanation of miracle which does not really succeed in getting rid of it."[10]

The key to a true solution, or synthesis, according to Strauss, was to challenge the premise which was the basic assumption of both the orthodox and the rationalists, namely, that the Gospels are reliable historical records. The Gospels, Strauss insisted, in opposition to the rationalists, are not merely inaccurate descriptions of historical events. They are descriptions of events that, for the most part, never happened at all. The gospel accounts are, through and through, myths.

---

[9]Schweitzer notes that Schleiermacher was the first theologian who had ever lectured on the life of Jesus (in 1819). But his lectures on that subject were not published until 1864, when, as a result of Strauss's criticism in the intervening years, "Schleiermacher's work was brought forth to view like an embalmed corpse" (*The Quest of the Historical Jesus,* trans. W. Montgomery, 2d ed. [1911; reprint, London: Adam & Charles Black, 1945], 62).

[10]Schweitzer, *Quest of the Historical Jesus,* 63.

Strauss was not the originator of the theory of myth. Christian Gottlob Heyne (1729–1812) had developed a comprehensive theory of the origin and nature of myth as "the universal mode of thinking and expression in humanity's infancy."[11] Johann Gottfried Eichhorn (1752–1827) had applied Heyne's theory to the first three chapters of Genesis, and Johann Philipp Gabler (1753–1826) had introduced the concept of myth into New Testament studies. But Strauss did the previously unthinkable by applying the concept of myth to the entire narrative of the Gospels, including even their basic historical framework.

Strauss professed to be surprised and deeply hurt by the fierce negative reaction received by his book—from rationalists and liberals as well as from the orthodox. He claimed that he had not conceived of his proposal as an attempt to undermine Christianity. His goal was rather to make the Christian faith intelligible, and therefore credible, to post-Enlightenment men and women. *Myth* is not a pejorative term, Strauss insisted.[12] Myth is not to be viewed as a distortion of the essential gospel message but rather as the communicative medium of that message.

Here is where Strauss's Hegelian roots are exposed.[13] A myth, as Strauss presented the concept, may be defined as an idea clothed in the form of history. Hegel had stressed the need to distinguish between the Idea *(Begriff)* and the Form *(Vorstellung),* which is the historical representation of the Idea at a particular stage in history. Since the Idea is the important thing, we may, at no loss, dispense with the particular Form in which the Idea is presented at a particular time in history.

Religion, according to Hegel, and Christianity in particular (as the highest form of religion), expresses the very same Ideas that had come to their perfect expression in Hegelian philosophy, except that Christianity expresses them in symbolic and earthly terms—or, as Strauss would say, in myths. Those religious representations were

---

[11]Edwina G. Lawler, *David Friedrich Strauss and His Critics* (New York: Peter Lang, 1986), 23.

[12]Strauss spoke of the Gospel myths as "unintentional" or "unconscious fiction" (*Life of Jesus,* 82–83).

[13]"Here, at the outset, the general character of the gospels was less a literary discovery than a deduction from Hegel" (Ben F. Meyer, *The Aims of Jesus* [London: SCM, 1979], 34).

suitable, even helpful perhaps, at an earlier stage of man's development. Now, however, we must grow beyond that stage by demythologizing the truths of Christianity and demonstrating that the historic representations in the Gospels are simply imperfect representations of the eternal Ideas of reason.

The God-man concept, for example, is an especially high concept in the history of religion. This Idea came to expression historically and most vividly in Christianity. The validity of the Idea, however, is in no way dependent upon the validity of the historic expression. The important thing is that the fruitful Idea has entered the world.

Indeed, the Christian doctrine of the Incarnation is not only imperfect, but dangerously imperfect, because it masks the fact that the divine comes to self-expression in humanity as a whole, not only in one particular individual. Therefore, it is vitally important to demonstrate the mythical nature of the particular history recorded in the Gospels in order to free the Idea of the God-man from its attachment to one person only. The myth of the Incarnation can be seen as true only if it is seen as a symbol of the truth concerning mankind, not one individual man. The Cross is to be seen as a symbol of the Infinite's giving itself up in finitude, while the Resurrection symbolizes the ultimate and "perfect accomplishment of the Absolute as totally reconciling infinite Spirit."[14]

In his lengthy introduction, Strauss distinguishes various kinds of myths.[15] In the Gospels there are, on the one hand, "historical" myths, which had some real event as their "trigger," but which are now, in the form in which they appear in our Gospels, thoroughly transformed by mythical conceptions arising from the theological understanding of Jesus Christ as the God-man. On the other hand, the Gospels also contain "philosophical" myths, the most pure form of myth, in which the idea constitutes the entire substance of the narrative and the historical element is negligible or nonexistent.

It should be emphasized again that Strauss did not view the creation of the gospel myths as the result of fraud or a desire to deceive (compare Reimarus), nor as the result of faulty observation (Paulus).

---

[14]Masterson, *Atheism and Alienation,* 55.
[15]See Strauss, *Life of Jesus,* 52–53 and 86–87 in particular.

How, then, did they originate? How was it possible for these myths to be recorded and believed? Strauss pointed to many factors:

1. We must keep in mind, according to Strauss, that the Gospels were not written by the disciples of Jesus. They are not eyewitness accounts, and therefore are not reliable history. (On this point, the views of later students of the Gospels have run strongly counter to Strauss's opinion. Strauss held to a late date, a second-century date, for the writing of the Gospels. Today the dates most commonly proposed for the writing of the Gospels range between A.D. 60 and 95.[16])

2. We must recognize, Strauss continually emphasized, the powerful influence of the messianic expectations then current among the Jews. Since Moses and the prophets performed miracles (both Elijah and Elisha, for example, raised the dead), the Messiah was expected to perform even more miracles—and even more spectacular ones. Once Jesus was recognized by his followers as the Messiah, these popular expectations naturally came to be associated with him. *This argument is the cornerstone of Strauss's mythical interpretation of the Gospels.*

3. But Strauss also emphasized the overwhelming impression "left by the personal character, actions, and fate of Jesus."[17] The tremendous impact of Jesus' personality made it highly likely that messianic myths would be developed concerning him.

4. The resurrection was the key myth. Once it was believed that Jesus had been raised from the dead, anything could be believed about him.

We shall look at Strauss's influential theory concerning the origin of the resurrection myth soon, but first let us ask how the reader of a particular passage in the Gospels can determine whether what is spo-

---

[16]For even earlier dates, see especially John A. T. Robinson, *Redating the New Testament* (Philadelphia: Westminster, 1976), and John Wenham, *Redating Matthew, Mark and Luke* (Downer's Grove, Ill.: InterVarsity, 1992). Robinson argues that "the final stages of the three synoptic gospels as we have them would . . . have occupied the latter 50s or early 60s" (p. 116), and "50–55 [=] first edition of our present gospel [of John] in Asia Minor . . . 65+ [=] the final form of the gospel, with prologue and epilogue" (p. 307). Wenham puts forward what he terms the "radical thesis" that "all three [of the synoptics] are probably to be dated before 55" (p. xxii).

[17]Strauss, *Life of Jesus,* 86.

ken of there is historical or mythological. Strauss offers both negative and positive criteria.[18]

Negatively, (1) any narrative is unhistorical if it "is irreconcilable with the known and universal laws which govern the course of events." An absolute cause "never disturbs the chain of secondary causes by single arbitrary acts of interposition." In other words, when searching for the historical, begin by eliminating the supernatural. (2) A narrative is also unhistorical if it violates "all those psychological laws" regarding habit, memory, and human development. And finally, (3) the historicity of any recorded event must be tested by the self-consistency of the written account and its harmony with other accounts. (Logically, this third test, inconsistency in the accounts, would seem to prove at most that no more than one of the accounts could be true.)

Positively, (1) with regard to the form of the narrative, evidences of literary stylization (poetry) are indicative of a myth. (2) With regard to the substance of the narrative, wherever we can see the possible influence of prevailing, preconceived ideas (especially expectations regarding the coming Messiah), the historicity of the narrative immediately becomes suspect. The consequence of this criterion is that every fulfillment of prophecy must be viewed as mythical.

Strauss cautioned that each of these criteria, when applied in isolation, may leave the reader less than absolutely certain regarding the historicity of a particular event. But clearly, for Strauss, those who would affirm the historicity of the supernatural at any point bear an impossible burden of proof.

Strauss's own view of Jesus, the result of his application of the above criteria to the gospel accounts, was as follows: Jesus actually lived. He thought himself to be the Messiah, and his disciples accepted him as such. Although Jesus regarded himself as a mere human, he thought that in some sense he would return after his death to bring in the kingdom. Therefore, his hope was not merely political and earthly (Reimarus), but neither was it merely spiritual (Paulus and Schleiermacher). Strauss stated,

> Thus we conclude that the messianic hope of Jesus was not political, nor even merely earthly, for he referred its fulfillment to supernatural

---

[18]Ibid., 88–89.

means, and to a supermundane theatre (the regenerated earth): as little was it a purely spiritual hope, in the modern sense of the term, for it included important and unprecedented changes in the external condition of things: but it was the national, theocratic hope, spiritualized and ennobled by his own peculiar moral and religious views.[19]

Nothing recorded in the Gospels regarding Jesus' life before his baptism, Strauss concluded, has any historical basis at all. Certain healing miracles are explainable as psychosomatic cures. Here Strauss's suggestion is quite similar to the earlier rationalist treatments. But his explanation of the feeding of the five thousand is typical of his distinctively different approach to the so-called nature miracles. This story, according to Strauss, developed out of the acceptance of Jesus as the Messiah without any basis in historical fact. Jesus had indeed given certain discourses concerning bread (Matt. 16:5ff.; John 6). These discourses were misunderstood and literalized, but even more important was the fact that the Old Testament contains certain stories about miraculous provisions of food (such as the manna and the quail in answer to Moses' prayer, and the bread and meat provided for Elijah).

In other words, analogous events in the ministries of God's servants in the Old Covenant, of which the evangelical preacher might well remind his congregation in order to deepen their appreciation of Jesus' miracle as confirming him as the servant of God commissioned to establish the New Covenant, Strauss points to in order to explain the origin of this miracle story.

Especially important is Strauss's theory of the origin of the resurrection myth, because it has been adopted by many critics who have come after him. It is often referred to as "the Galilean hypothesis"; and it rests on the idea of "subjective visions," which, of course, is a theological euphemism for hallucinations. Strauss traced various stages in the development of the Easter faith:[20]

1. Faith in Jesus as the Messiah goes back to the ministry of Jesus itself.

2. Jesus' death "annihilated" this faith. In confusion, Jesus' disciples left Jerusalem and returned to Galilee.

---

[19]Ibid., 296.
[20]Ibid., 742.

3. There the disciples' fears began to dissipate, and their faith revived. Here would seem to be a problematic point for Strauss's theory. Why did the disciples' faith return in spite of their hero's death?

4. With their faith restored, there arose the psychological necessity for harmonizing their faith in him as Messiah with the fact of his death. This they accomplished by turning to the Old Testament. "Foreign as the idea of such a Messiah is to the Old Testament," Strauss writes, by the disciples who wished to see it there, the idea of a suffering and glorified Messiah could be found in such passages as Isaiah 53 and Psalm 22.

5. Thus the question naturally arose—and here is another point at which Strauss's theory seems particularly weak—How could the Christ have failed to give tidings to his followers out of his glory?

6. It is not surprising, Strauss insists—and "especially" not surprising for women!—that in this frame of mind the believers began to suffer subjective visions. First Corinthians 15 reveals how many firmly believed they had seen him. These visions actually occurred first in Galilee, but they were later transferred in the tradition to Jerusalem.

7. But if the Messiah had been taken up into glory, he ought not to have left his body in the grave. (Think, for example, of Ps. 16:10.) From this notion, according to Strauss, the totally unbelievable, obviously contradictory resurrection stories recorded in the Gospels developed. When the resurrection was later proclaimed in Jerusalem, there was no recognizable body available to refute the disciples' claim.

We have already noted that many consider Strauss to be the single most important figure in the history of Gospels criticism. That is why we have devoted so many pages to the exposition of his thought. Orthodox Christians in Strauss's day expressed a certain appreciation for his effective, at some points devastating, attacks on the earlier rationalism[21] and gave him credit for at least taking a more *consistently* unbelieving position. More recent gospel critics, however—Rudolf Bultmann, for example— have tried to take the notion of myth, which Strauss introduced into the study of the Gospels, and apply it much more consistently than Strauss himself did. It is viewed as the grave weakness of Strauss's position, on

---

[21]"On the exegetical front he delivered the *coup de grace* to the school of Rationalism." Meyer, *Aims of Jesus,* 32.

his own presuppositions, that he "measures with two measures." He wants to have it both ways. On the one hand, he looked upon the church as virtually creating the Christianity we know today by creating the myths concerning Jesus Christ. (This is the radical emphasis in Gospels criticism.) At the same time, however, Strauss laid great weight on the extraordinary impact made by the words and works of Jesus of Nazareth and the force of his personality. (This is the liberal emphasis.) On Strauss's view, at least the original creative influence was Jesus himself. Thus, there must have been more continuity between Jesus himself and later church tradition than Strauss's overall position allows.

As Stephen Neill insists, however: "The kind of Jesus who is indicated in Strauss's pages was not the kind of person to create that kind of faith. The causes, as suggested by Strauss, do not measure up to the consequences; something in the evidence that is of the greatest significance must somehow have been overlooked."[22]

Many contemporary New Testament critics, however, unwilling to consider the possibility that what was overlooked by Strauss was that Jesus was indeed that unique person (the incarnate Son of God) to whom the faith of the church points, suggest that Strauss's mistake was that he was not nearly radical enough. They seek to be more consistently radical than Strauss by eliminating the creative significance of Jesus from the history entirely.

2. Bruno Bauer (1809–82)

With regard to the other two disciples of Hegel to be considered in this chapter, we can be much briefer. Reference to Bruno Bauer is made at this point simply to indicate that at least one Hegelian New Testament scholar in the mid-nineteenth century was willing to take the most radical position possible with regard to the historicity of the Gospels and the creative role of Jesus in the origin of Christianity. He denied that Jesus ever lived!

Bruno Bauer, along with Karl Marx and others, was a member of the so-called Young Hegelians, or the Hegelians of the Left. Another

---

[22]Neill and Wright, *Interpretation of the New Testament,* 19.

prominent member of that group, Friedrich Engels, wrote an essay on "Bruno Bauer and Early Christianity," on the occasion of Bauer's death in Berlin on April 13, 1882, praising the significance of his colleague's contribution to the history of Western thought.[23]

Engels acknowledges with regret that Bauer was almost completely ignored in his time, but he insists that Bauer was "worth more" than all the other New Testament scholars combined, "and did more than all of them in a question which interests us socialists too: the question of the historical origin of Christianity." Bauer offered an exclusively sociological explanation for the origin of the Christian church and for the tradition about Jesus as the product of the church's communal consciousness. Engels writes:

> A religion that brought the Roman world empire into subjection and dominated by far the larger part of civilized humanity for 1,800 years cannot be disposed of merely by declaring it to be nonsense gleaned together by frauds. One cannot dispose of it before one succeeds in explaining its origin and its development from the historical conditions under which it arose and reached its dominating position. . . . The question to be solved, then, is how it came about that the popular masses in the Roman Empire so far preferred this nonsense—which was preached, into the bargain, by slaves and oppressed—to all other religions that the ambitious Constantine finally saw in the adoption of this religion of nonsense the best means of exalting himself to the position of autocrat of the Roman world.

The fundamental Marxist thesis is that "religions are founded by people who feel a need for religion themselves and have a feeling for the religious needs of the masses." Bauer was the first to demonstrate clearly, according to Engels, that Christianity appeared in the midst of the "general economic, political, intellectual and moral decadence" of the first century and "struck a chord that was bound to echo in countless hearts."

Whereas Strauss considered himself a friend of Christianity,

---

[23]Karl Marx and Friedrich Engels, *On Religion* (Moscow: Progress Publishers, 1975), 170–79. The quotations from Engels's essay that follow are from pages 170, 171, 172, 177, and 178. Some of Bauer's writings can be found today only at the University of Moscow.

Bruno Bauer was vehemently anti-Christian. All the Gospels, he insisted, were merely literary fiction with no history behind them at all. There never was such a person as Jesus of Nazareth.

On the post-Enlightenment presuppositions of radical Gospels criticism, this notion is not as irrational as one might suppose. Indeed, Bauer's denial of the historicity of Jesus might well be considered the *reductio ad absurdum* of the radical position. We shall see later that it was the dissatisfaction of some of Bultmann's students with what Bultmann's criticism had left them of a historical Jesus (very little!) that caused them to embark on the so-called new quest. The more gospel tradition that one assigns to the Christian community for its origin, the less there remains of solid evidence for Jesus' life, and the less one needs Jesus to explain the origin of Christianity.

Early in the twentieth century, fifty years and more after Bauer's proposal,[24] many books were written by scholars in many countries in defense of Bauer's thesis.[25] These books represented a reaction against the popular, liberal "lives of Jesus" and a sympathy for the rising tide of socialism and communism. The historicity of Jesus was defended mostly by liberals. Orthodox Christians did not get very excited about this movement. The position of Bauer and his followers was so obviously altogether speculative that orthodox Christians felt no great need to answer it. Virtually no one today denies the historicity of Jesus.

3. Ferdinand Christian Baur (1792–1860)

Ferdinand Christian Baur is an important name in the history of biblical criticism.[26] He was the head of the celebrated "Tübingen school,"

---

[24]In his first publication, *A Critique of Gospel History* (1841–42), the work that cost him his academic position, Bauer denied the historicity of Jesus' messianic consciousness, but he still accepted the historicity of Jesus' person. It was in *A Critique of the Gospels* (1850–51) that Bauer denied the historicity of Jesus altogether.

[25]For example, from Scotland: John M. Robertson, *Christianity and Mythology* (London: Watts & Co., 1900); from Germany: Arthur Drews, *Die Christusmythe* (Jena: E. Diederichs, 1909); from Denmark: Georg Brandes, *Jesus, a Myth,* trans. Edwin Björkman (New York: Boni, 1926).

[26]Baur published many works. Two that are available in English are *Paul, the Apostle of Jesus Christ, His Life and Work, His Epistles and Teachings,* 2d ed., ed.

which ruled biblical scholarship in the mid-nineteenth century. So pervasive was its dominance, that the later part of the century has been described as the period of "the gradual de-Tübingenizing of New Testament studies."

Baur concentrated his attention on the origin of the New Testament writings, which he considered to be the grave lack in Strauss's work. He constructed a Hegelian, dialectical interpretation of the development of early Christianity, which posited a deep-seated conflict between a Jewish Christianity and a Pauline Christianity, and saw a synthesis being reached in the middle of the second century. This conflict arose within the apostolic circle itself, according to Baur, as Paul's letter to the Galatians shows us.

It is therefore possible, Baur insisted, to date all the books of the New Testament according to the point of view expressed in each and its place in this dialectical historical development. Matthew is a Jewish-Christian document and thus the earliest gospel. Pauline Christianity is represented by Romans, 1 and 2 Corinthians, and Galatians. The remaining New Testament books (Mark, John, Luke, Acts, Hebrews, the other letters, including those attributed to Paul) reflect the synthesis, compromise viewpoint that developed after A.D. 150 and thus were written at a very late date.

In contrast to Strauss, Baur spoke of the Gospels as containing not unconscious but *conscious* fiction. Every New Testament document was a "party document," representing a particular partisan position in the early church. The term associated with the Tübingen school of interpretation is the German word *Tendenz*, meaning "tendency." The word has a negative connotation, much like our English word *propaganda*. The *Tendenz* of a writing is its partisan view.[27]

Baur presented a very negative estimate of the Gospel of John, and in this respect he was very influential on later thinking. If we

Eduard Zeller, trans. Allan Menzies, 2 vols. (London: Williams and Norgate, 1873–75); and *The Church History of the First Centuries,* 3d ed., trans. and ed. Allan Menzies, 2 vols. (London: Williams and Norgate, 1878–79).

[27]Baur's enthusiasm for discovering the underlying *Tendenz* of every historical source was probably the result of his study of Barthold Georg Niebuhr's *Römische Geschichte* [Roman history], 2 vols. (Berlin: G. Reimer, 1811–12).

take the Gospel of John at face value, Baur stressed, we must recognize that it is speaking of an incarnation of deity, and thus in this
book we are obviously beyond the realm of history. For Baur, as
for the later critics, the factual value of the Fourth Gospel was rejected because of its content, not because of its authorship, the manu-
script evidence, or the like. The historicity of this gospel was rejected not on historical grounds, but on philosophical (theological)
ones.

Strauss did not distinguish so sharply between John and the
synoptics with regard to historical trustworthiness. As Strauss saw
them, all four gospels present a thoroughly supernatural Christ—even
Mark, which has often been considered to be the most "simple"
gospel. On this point, as well as others, the later Ritschlian liberals
followed Baur, whereas later radical critics have tended to follow
Strauss.

Baur considered the Gospel of Mark to have been written very
late, because it represents the time of synthesis and accommodation.
This explains, according to Baur, its bland and colorless content. The
author of this gospel wanted to avoid the earlier controversies in the
church. There had been contradictory traditions, for example, regarding Jesus' birth. Mark's solution was simply to include no birth narrative at all.

With regard to the relation of Mark to the other gospels, Baur has
been followed by neither the liberal nor the radical critics, most of
whom have affirmed the priority of Mark. Certainly it is interesting,
and instructive, to observe what widely differing conclusions arise
from attempts first to reconstruct speculatively the history of doctrinal
development in the church, and then on that basis to put in order and
date the New Testament books. The circular tendency of such a methodology seems apparent.

Baur dated the Gospel of Matthew close to the middle of the
second century, and yet he considered it to be the earliest gospel—our
earliest representative of Jewish Christianity—and therefore the most
historically dependable of all our New Testament books. Baur based
his own Christian faith on certain portions of this gospel, namely, the
Beatitudes and some of the parables.

In his theology Baur anticipated later liberalism in many respects. He defined religion as the coming to consciousness of the universal moral idea. The task of the Christian theologian therefore (for example, in studying the letters of Paul) is "to separate the essential and universal from the less essential, the fortuitous . . ."[28] In Christianity the "high and absolute" religion,

> It is a truly spiritual consciousness, a relation of spirit to spirit, where the absolute spirit of God, in becoming the principle of the Christian consciousness, opens itself up to the consciousness of man.[29]

> In his Christian consciousness as an essentially spiritual one, the Christian knows himself to be identical with the spirit of God; for only the spirit, the spirit of God, the absolute spirit, can know the divine contents of the Christian consciousness.[30]

Thus, the Christian religion is not unique. In its original essence, Christianity came in the form of an absolute moral command. (Note the echo of Kant's categorical imperative of duty.) Jesus' value lay in his teaching us that we humans have the full ability to recognize and to obey this moral command and to attain righteousness. His aim was only to throw men and women back onto full dependence on their own innate moral and religious consciousness. His teaching was purely and exclusively moral, emphasizing his hearers' moral ability.

Jesus' concept of the kingdom of God was thus interpreted by Baur in exclusively human-centered terms. The kingdom of God is found where every individual feels himself required, with the force of an absolute moral command, to fulfill God's will. It is not merely an individual phenomenon, however, because the members of this kingdom are also to cooperate with one another to realize the goals that the will of God sets before them.

Baur emphasizes, however, that if this had been all that the Christian religion had offered, it would have had no appreciable impact on the world. It had to have a point of contact with the age to

---

[28]Baur, *Paul,* 2:115.
[29]Ibid., 128
[30]Ibid.

which it came. This was found in the historical Form in which its moral Idea came to expression. (Note the use of the Hegelian distinction between the *Begriff* and the *Vorstellung*.) It was the then-popular expectation of the Messiah that gave the moral Idea its attractive, concrete Form. So prevalent and so popular was this messianic concept among the religious people of that generation, that it *had* to be utilized if the moral Idea was to take root in history. Faith in Jesus had such power in the Jewish world because it was faith in him as the Messiah.

Jesus himself, Baur said, must have availed himself of this popular concept that lay so readily at hand, and indeed Jesus must have come to think of himself as the Messiah. His use of the title Son of Man, his acceptance of Peter's confession at Caesarea Phillippi, and his royal entry into Jerusalem convinced Baur of Jesus' own messianic consciousness.

Because of Jesus' death, however, there came a complete break between him and Judaism. If faith in Jesus were to survive, that faith had to burst through death itself and break forth into life. Baur was typical of liberal theologians generally in being quite vague at this crucial point. He stressed that nothing but the miracle of the Resurrection could erase the disciples' doubts. The fact of the resurrection of Jesus, however, lies outside the realm of historical inquiry. All we can say is that faith in the Resurrection was the foundation of Christianity. That faith became the important thing in history, whether there was fact behind it or not.

But even those two elements, according to Baur—the moral Idea and its historical Form of a resurrected Messiah—would not have sufficed to work the miracle of Christianity. By themselves, they would have produced at best only a stronger modification of the Jewish messianic faith, and the church would have remained merely a Jewish sect. Everything had to be raised to the higher plane of a truly universal religion. This, said Baur, was the great contribution of the Pauline expression of Christianity. The long struggle between the original, Jewish-Christian outlook and the Pauline outlook was ultimately resolved in the concept of the Catholic church.

The significance of F. C. Baur in the history of Gospels criticism, which is so closely linked with the history of Protestant theology, is that he was one of the important forerunners of liberalism.[31] He might very well have been included, therefore, under our next topic, "Ritschlian Liberalism—Transition Period." Let us move on, then, to that significant chapter in our history.

---

[31]This is not to suggest that with the decline of liberalism in the twentieth century, Baur's influence has totally disappeared. Stephen Neill makes the interesting comment that "one of the curious features in German theology is that no ghost is ever laid. A century after his death Baur still walks abroad, and echoes of his ideas are found in all kinds of places." Neill and Wright, *Interpretation of the New Testament,* 62.

3

Ritschlian Liberalism

CONSERVATIVE, evangelical Christians today often use the term *liberal* in a broad sense to refer to the whole range of nonorthodox Christian thought. In the history of theology, however, the term is also used in a more narrow and specific sense to refer to a particular school of Protestant thought that arose in the late nineteenth century. Theological liberals have been distinguished by their keen interest in the historical Jesus and the high religious value that they place upon him and his teachings.

1. Transitional Period

The three principal characteristics of Gospels criticism in the period immediately leading up to liberalism (roughly the middle of the nineteenth century) were these:

1. The rejection of "Tübingenism." We have said that the positive theology of the leading Tübingen scholar, F. C. Baur, anticipated liberalism. At the same time, however, the period of transition to liberalism was marked by either a moderation or an outright rejection

of the Tübingen reconstruction of early church history and its dating of the New Testament books.

2. A tendency toward a thoroughly noneschatological, moralistic interpretation of Jesus and his teaching concerning the kingdom of God.

3. The development of source criticism, concerned most especially with the origin of the gospel documents, focusing on the literary materials used in their composition.

It was during this period that what soon came to be the most widely accepted theory of synoptic gospel origins,[1] known as the Marcan hypothesis, was developed by such scholars as the philologist Karl Lachmann,[2] the philosopher Christian Hermann Weisse,[3] and the New Testament professor Heinrich Julius Holtzmann.[4]

C. H. Weisse (1801–66) was rationalistic, naturalistic, and speculative—but not Hegelian. It was he who proposed all the essentials of the so-called Marcan hypothesis, also known as "the two-document hypothesis" of gospel origins. The two fundamental documents lying behind the Synoptic Gospels were thought to be Mark, considered to be the first of our gospels to be written, and another source, made up largely of a collection of Jesus' sayings and usually referred to as Q, from the first letter of the German word *Quelle* ("source"). This hypothetical Q was later reconstructed on the basis of sayings of Jesus that are common to Matthew and Luke but (usu-

---

[1]The familiar term *synoptic,* as a designation of the first three canonical gospels, goes back to the textual critic Johann Jakob Griesbach (1745–1812). In order to more easily compare the texts of Matthew, Mark, and Luke—highlighting both their striking agreements and their differences—he had these three gospels printed in parallel columns (with their parallel passages side by side) in a "synopsis" (our technical term still for such an arrangement of closely corresponding texts).

[2]Karl Lachmann, "De ordine narrationum in evangeliis synopticis" [The order of the narratives in the Synoptic Gospels], *Theologische Studien und Kritiken* 8 (1835): 570ff.

[3]C. H. Weisse, *Die evangelische Geschichte, kritisch und philosophisch bearbeitet* [The gospel history treated critically and philosophically], 2 vols. (Leipzig: Breitkopf und Härtel, 1838).

[4]H. J. Holtzmann, *Die synoptischen Evangelien: Ihr Ursprung und geschichtlicher Charakter* [The Synoptic Gospels: their origin and historical character] (Leipzig: W. Engelmann, 1863), and *Die Synoptiker* (Freiburg: J. C. B. Mohr, 1889).

ally) not found in Mark.[5] On this hypothesis, as originally presented, Mark was viewed not only as the earliest of our canonical gospels, but also as the most historically reliable gospel.

Weisse was also influential in his understanding of Jesus' messianic consciousness. Jesus' own concept of his messianic task, Weisse insisted, was thoroughly noneschatological. Certain of Jesus' sayings

---

[5]The definitive German statement of this theory was presented by Paul Wernle in *Die synoptische Frage* (Freiburg: J. C. B. Mohr, 1899). To say that the two-document hypothesis came to be, and continues to be, the most widely held theory of synoptic gospel origins is not to say that it has had no opponents or that no other theory has been presented. Both Marcan priority and the very existence of Q have been challenged. See Stephen Neill and Tom Wright, *The Interpretation of the New Testament 1861–1986,* 2d ed. (Oxford: Oxford University Press, 1988), 362. E. Earle Ellis writes with tongue in cheek about essays which continue to be written "purporting to set forth the hypothetical theology of the hypothetical community of the hypothetical document Q," and states his opinion that "it is probable that the non-Marcan material common to Matthew and Luke comes from more than one written source" ("Gospels Criticism: A Perspective on the State of the Art," *The Gospel and the Gospels,* ed. Peter Stuhlmacher [Grand Rapids: Eerdmans, 1991], 34, 36).

Too often, students see such frequent references to Q that they tend to forget that this document is completely hypothetical. Some have even gone to the library to check out a copy of Q! And, sure enough, they find it—in several different texts and translations! Four recent examples are (1) *Q: The Sayings of Jesus,* by the Roman Catholic scholar Ivan Havener (Wilmington: Michael Glazier, 1987), which includes a translation of Athanasius Polag's "reconstruction . . . of the text of Q, as it was used by Matthew and Luke in the composition of their Gospels" (p. 11)—now, that's confidence! (2) *Q Parallels,* by John S. Kloppenborg (Sonoma, Calif.: Polebridge, 1988); (3) *Q-Thomas Reader*, by John S. Kloppenborg et al. (Sonoma, Calif.: Polebridge, 1990); and (4) *The Lost Gospel,* by Burton L. Mack (San Francisco: Harper San Francisco, 1993).

The so-called two-gospel hypothesis, which goes back to J. J. Griesbach (and even earlier) and often bears his name (see footnote 1, above), asserts that Matthew was the first gospel written, that Luke used Matthew, and that Mark used both Matthew and Luke. This theory has seen a certain revival in the past generation, through such studies as Hans-Herbert Stoldt, *History and Criticism of the Marcan Hypothesis,* trans. Donald L. Niewyk (Macon, GA.: Mercer University Press, 1980), and William R. Farmer, *The Synoptic Problem* (New York: Macmillan, 1964). See also M.-E. Boismard, "The Two-Source Theory at an Impasse," *New Testament Studies* 26 (1980): 1–17; G. M. Styler, "The Priority of Mark," in *The Birth of the New Testament,* ed. C. F. D. Moule, 3d ed. (San Francisco: Harper & Row, 1981), 285–316; William R. Farmer, ed., *New Synoptic Studies* (Macon, Ga.: Mercer University Press, 1983), and C. M. Tuckett, *The Revival of the Griesbach Hypothesis* (New York: Cambridge University Press, 1983).

came to be given a literal interpretation by his disciples that Jesus himself could never have intended. Weisse was convinced that the Jesus whose ethical and religious teaching he admired so much could have taken no part in such fantastic errors. Jesus' predictions of his coming resurrection must have meant only that his spirit would live on. In *The Quest of the Historical Jesus,* Albert Schweitzer really lambastes Weisse and the later liberals for their subjective making over of Jesus in their own image.[6]

H. J. Holtzmann (1832–1910), professor of New Testament first at Heidelberg and then for thirty years at Strassburg, was one of the most influential professors in the German-speaking world. Early in his teaching career, he was quite radical in his criticism of the Gospels, but he came to be greatly influenced by the newly emerging trends of his age—evolutionary theory and theological liberalism. In his 1863 book on synoptic origins, he strongly supported the Marcan hypothesis—both Mark's priority and Mark's relatively high historical reliability. On the basis of Mark's Gospel, Holtzmann thought that he could reconstruct in some detail the life of the historical Jesus, and in his book he included a twenty-page outline of the course of Jesus' life.

In this he was a strong influence upon later writers. A flood of life-of-Jesus books appeared in the latter half of the nineteenth century. Evolutionism had captured the imagination of many, and Darwinian principles were being applied to virtually every field of study (for example, by Karl Marx to history and economics, and by Herbert Spencer to ethics, sociology, psychology, and politics). Men and women seemed virtually possessed by the idea of development and progress. Holtzmann thought, for example, that he could find seven distinct stages in Jesus' Galilean ministry, and that he could trace the progressive development of the messianic idea in particular in the consciousness of Jesus. Today it is universally recognized that there is no evidence of such development in the Gospels themselves.[7]

---

[6]Pp. 134, 136.

[7]Especially helpful in this regard is the brief chapter 6, "The Theory of Development of Jesus into the Messianic Consciousness," in Geerhardus Vos, *The Self-disclosure of Jesus,* ed. Johannes G. Vos (Grand Rapids: Eerdmans, 1954), 88–94.

2. Albrecht Ritschl (1822–89)

To make it clear that they are referring not to theological liberalism in general, but to the particular school of liberal theology that arose in Germany in the late nineteenth century and gained acceptance by so many Protestants throughout the world, historians of Christian doctrine often speak of Ritschlian liberalism. It was this liberalism, or modernism, against which orthodox Christians did battle in the United States in the first three decades of this century.[8]

The professor who gave his name to this movement, Albrecht Ritschl, began his academic career as a Hegelian and a disciple of F. C. Baur at Tübingen, but he first rose to prominence as Baur's most effective critic.[9] Although an adherent of the Tübingen school of New Testament and early church studies for some eleven years, Ritschl eventually came to believe that Baur had made three basic mistakes: (1) The New Testament does not bear witness to an antithesis within the apostolic circle. In the letter to the Galatians, it is not a matter of Paul versus Peter, but rather Paul versus the Judaizers.[10] (2) Baur greatly exaggerated the influence of Jewish Christianity. That influ-

---

[8]This theological (and ecclesiastical) battle in the 1920s is often referred to as the fundamentalist-modernist controversy. The term *fundamentalism* goes back to the publication between 1910 and 1915 of a series of twelve paperback volumes containing essays in defense of the "fundamental" doctrines of the Christian faith, written by a wide variety of American and British theological conservatives, both premillennialists and nonpremillennialists. See Ernest R. Sandeen, *The Roots of Fundamentalism* (Chicago: University of Chicago Press, 1970), 188–207.

J. Gresham Machen's *Christianity and Liberalism* (New York: Macmillan, 1923) remains the most effective critique of this theological liberalism. The title itself indicates Machen's basic thesis: that this modernism was not a form of Christianity, but a new religion.

[9]For a detailed account of Ritschl's relationship with Baur, including helpful bibliographical references, see Horton Harris, *The Tübingen School* (Oxford: Clarendon, 1975), 101–12.

[10]Neill credits J. B. Lightfoot's study of Clement and Ignatius in *Apostolic Fathers* (New York: Macmillan, 1891) with causing "the whole mythology of the enmity between Peter and Paul, of the later reconciliation in the church, and of the dating of New Testament books in the middle of the second century" to collapse "like a house of cards" (Neill and Wright, *Interpretation of the New Testament,* 60). But Ritschl had begun the destruction of the Tübingen positions many years earlier with the publication

ence had virtually come to an end by A.D. 70. (3) Baur's dating of the
New Testament books on the basis of the *Tendenz* found in each was
on shaky ground, and the actual evidence points to a much more
conservative dating of the documents.

Having begun as a New Testament scholar, and then focusing on
church history, from 1852 onwards Ritschl was a professor of dogmatics (systematic theology), teaching at Göttingen from 1864 until his
death. It is as the father of an important theological movement, not as
a Gospels critic, that Ritschl is a significant figure in the history of
Gospels criticism.

There is a basic agnosticism running throughout the whole of
Ritschl's theology, as well as a strongly Kantian distinction between
scientific knowledge and religious knowledge. Although he had been
influenced earlier by both Schleiermacher and Hegel, Ritschl rejected
both Schleiermacher's appeal to the subjective and mystical and Hegel's
appeal to philosophy and metaphysics as the final judge of what is real.
Against Schleiermacher, Ritschl emphasized the historical basis of Christian faith in the person and work of Jesus of Nazareth. Against Hegel—
and Christian orthodoxy—Ritschl emphasized the nonmetaphysical character of doctrinal statements.

In Ritschl's estimation, religious affirmations—regarding God,
for example—are strictly "value judgments." That qualifier, "value,"
cuts two ways: a value judgment is a judgment that affirms what we
consider to be of value for our life; at the same time, it is a judgment
that actually has value in making our life the kind of life it should be.
A person can come to a sense of his or her own dignity and worth
through the idea of a God who is his or her Creator, Savior, and
Sustainer. But remember, Ritschl emphasized that this doctrine of a
divine being is strictly a value judgment. And the only concept of
God that can pass the test of being a value(able) judgment is one in
which God is exclusively love—not holiness, not justice, not judgment.

The same polemic against the metaphysical controlled Ritschl's
treatment of the person of Jesus Christ. Ritschl emphatically repudiated

---

of the second edition of his *Die Entstehung der altkatholischen Kirche* [The rise of the
ancient Catholic Church] (Bonn: A. Marcus, 1857).

the orthodox doctrine of Christ's two natures, yet he retained the traditional terms, such as *deity,* in order to express the value, the unique value, of Jesus' life for us. As the founder of Christianity, Jesus Christ has for Christians the value of God. "You ask what Jesus means to me," Ritschl would say; "well, he stands so preeminently at the very center of my religious and ethical life that for me—there is no other way to express it adequately—he has the religious and ethical value of God!"[11] Nothing but a confession of his deity will do justice to the mission Jesus accomplished in the world.[12] He is the prototype of morally perfect humanity and the one in whom God reveals himself as love.

In contrast to Strauss and Baur, for whom Ideas alone are of ultimate importance, Ritschl was vitally concerned with history, and especially with the history of Jesus. This particular history, even though it is a purely human history, can have religious value, even revelational value, for us.

The heart of Ritschl's positive theology was the concept of the kingdom of God, which he interpreted solely in ethical and social terms. The kingdom comes as men unite for common moral action, motivated by love.[13] Christianity he defined as the absolutely ethical religion. As H. R. Macintosh has described it, Ritschl's "view of

---

[11]Christians have often puzzled over how it can be that although the Basis of the World Council of Churches, to which all member churches express agreement, affirms that "the World Council of Churches is a fellowship of churches which confess the Lord Jesus Christ as God and Saviour," the WCC has admitted into membership some churches that clearly do not confess the deity of Christ. As a WCC publication makes clear: "The WCC respects the freedom of its member churches to interpret this and other affirmations in the Basis according to their own teachings" (Marlin Van Elderen, *Introducing the World Council of Churches* [Geneva: WCC Publications, 1990], 6). Understanding Ritschl's concept of doctrinal pronouncements as "value judgments" helps us understand one way in which certain modern Christians and churches interpret the WCC affirmation.

[12]Albrecht Benjamin Ritschl, *The Christian Doctrine of Justification and Reconciliation,* trans. and ed. H. R. Mackintosh and A. B. Macaulay (Edinburgh: T. & T. Clark, 1900), 389.

[13]The social gospel movement, which was influential in the United States at the close of the nineteenth century and the beginning of the twentieth, and whose foremost exponent was the Baptist theologian Walter Rauschenbusch, flowed naturally from Ritschl's teaching.

religion as such is utilitarian and intramundane. . . . [R]eligion has emerged as a product of the struggle for existence. . . . God is the needed prop of ethical aspiration, the trustee of our moral interests."[14]

In other words, God is a value(able) judgment. The kingdom that Ritschl envisioned involved no eschatological, extramundane reality; thus, it had no need for a personal, sovereign God and Savior.

3. Adolf von Harnack (1851–1930)

Ritschl had an immediate impact. A Ritschlian school of thought quickly developed, and for many years Ritschlian theology reigned, especially in Germany. There were many influential spokesmen for this liberal theology. One of the most brilliant was Wilhelm Herrmann (1846–1922) of Marburg, under whom many future theological leaders studied, including Karl Barth, Rudolf Bultmann—and J. Gresham Machen, who was so influential later in the battle for the orthodox Christian faith and in the founding of Westminster Theological Seminary.[15]

---

[14]H. R. Macintosh, *Types of Modern Theology* (London: Collins, 1964), 148.

[15]Too often, perhaps, later evangelical Christians have forgotten how attractively this "new" liberal theology could be presented by its most effective teachers. A poignant, and perhaps surprising, letter from Machen to his father reveals something of the mental turmoil of the young student, who seemed almost in danger of being swept off his orthodox feet by the powerful impact of his professor. Machen wrote:

> I can't criticize him [Herrmann], as my chief feeling with reference to him is already one of the deepest reverence. Since I have been listening to him, my other studies have for a time lost interest to me; for Herrmann refuses to allow the student to look at religion from a distance as a thing to be *studied* merely. He speaks right to the heart; and I have been thrown all into confusion by what he says—so much deeper is his devotion to Christ than anything I have known in myself during the past few years. I don't know at all what to say as yet, for Herrmann's views are so revolutionary. But certain I am that he has found Christ; and I believe that he can show how others may find Him—though, perhaps afterwards, in details, he may not be a safe guide. In fact, I am rather sorry I have said even so much in a letter; for I don't know at all yet what to think. (Ned B. Stonehouse, *J. Gresham Machen: A Biographical Memoir* [Grand Rapids: Eerdmans, 1955], 106)

It was in the teaching of Adolf von Harnack, however, that Ritschlian liberalism reached its high point. Harnack was a prolific and wide-ranging writer, producing major studies in New Testament, theology, and church history.

As an indication of his popularity as a lecturer, the story has been told of the first time, in the winter semester of 1899–1900, that he offered the lectures that became his most influential book. In the scheduling of classes at the University of Berlin at that time, professors got to choose when their courses would meet, each teacher getting his turn to choose according to his place in the faculty pecking order. As the newest professor at the university, Harnack could arrange no better hour for his course than 7:00 A.M.! Soon, however, his students had so spread the word concerning these remarkable lectures, that attendance had risen to over six hundred! Notes were taken on the lectures (which evidently were delivered extemporaneously) and published almost at once. By 1927 there were already fourteen German printings and translations into fourteen other languages. A new German edition was published in 1950 (later translated into English) with a commendatory introduction by Rudolf Bultmann.[16] (Stephen Neill comments on the "rather unexpected" nature of this tribute, since Bultmann's "ideas were very different from those of Harnack."[17] We shall see later why Neill says that Bultmann's ideas were so different, but it would seem that Bultmann's introduction to Harnack's book is a significant reminder that at root—in terms of their naturalistic presuppositions—the approaches they took to the Gospels were not really so different after all.)

For the book, which was intended as a popular rather than a scholarly work, Harnack chose the same title that Feuerbach had used for his influential atheistic polemic, *Das Wesen des Christentums* (a fact hidden in the English editions, which translate Feuerbach's title as "The Essence of Christianity," but Harnack's title as "What Is Chris-

---

[16]Adolf Harnack, *What Is Christianity?* trans. Thomas Bailey Saunders (New York: Harper & Row, 1957). For both a reflection on the excitement caused by Harnack's lectures when they were first published and a powerful critique of the theology presented in them, see James Orr, *Ritschlianism: Expository and Critical Essays* (London: Hodder and Stoughton, 1903), 115–48.

[17]Neill and Wright, *Interpretation of the New Testament,* 142.

tianity?"). Harnack's central thesis was that Christianity is not a matter of doctrine but of a life, kindled afresh again and again. What is distinctive about the Christian religion is the power of Jesus' contagious personality.

Although the Gospel of John must be rejected altogether as an historical source, the synoptics, Harnack believed, may be studied with some confidence. In *What Is Christianity?* Harnack spoke of Luke as probably having been written during the time of Domitian (the Roman emperor from 81 to 96), but he later argued strongly for the traditional dating of the gospel in the sixties and for Luke as its author.

With regard to the accounts of miracles in the synoptics, Harnack is reminiscent of Schleiermacher in his vagueness, and his treatment must be characterized as cavalier and totally unsatisfactory. Echoing Paulus, Harnack simply insists that "it is not miracles that matter."[18]

Unlike many other liberals (think back especially to Holtzmann), Harnack saw no discernible development in the gospel accounts of Jesus' life. Jesus consistently taught one message, a message that Harnack summarized in three points that have been frequently quoted ever since. Harnack stressed that each of these points is

> of such a nature as to contain the whole, and hence it [Jesus' teaching] can be exhibited in its entirety under any one of them.
> *Firstly, the kingdom of God and its coming.*
> *Secondly, God the Father and the infinite value of the human soul.*
> *Thirdly, the higher righteousness and the commandment of love.*[19]

There was an eschatological element in Jesus' message, Harnack admitted, but there was also this spiritual element, which was the higher element that had enduring significance. Jesus believed and said many things that have no relevance for our faith today. How are we to determine what in Jesus' teaching is of true religious significance? Harnack's famous criterion was this: those ideas that Jesus shared with his contemporaries are "husk," to be discarded (for example, the concept of a future, eternal kingdom); only that which was original with Jesus is "kernel" (for example, the concept of a present, internal

---

[18]Harnack, *What Is Christianity?* 30.
[19]Ibid., 51 (Harnack's italics).

kingdom). (Consider for a moment how you would like your own ideas to be judged on the basis of that criterion. Only those ideas that are unique to you, that are not shared by your contemporaries, are to be considered true! It should have been immediately obvious how unsatisfactory that standard is.)

Harnack insisted that "the whole of Jesus' message may be reduced to these two heads—God as the Father, and the human soul so ennobled that it can and does unite with him."[20] Clearly there is no good news for sinners here. Harnack had an utterly inadequate, Pelagian rather than biblical view of sin and of a sinner's need—and that led him to a lack of appreciation for Christ's work, and thus a lack of appreciation for his person.

Harnack explained the significance of Christ's death exclusively in terms of Abelard's moral influence theory: "It was by the cross of Jesus Christ that mankind gained such an experience of the power of purity and love true to death that they can never forget it."[21]

Although Harnack (like the other liberals) spoke of Jesus as the Son of God and believed (like F. C. Baur) that Jesus adopted the concept of messiahship as the best form then available in which to express his high sense of calling, he was quite explicit in teaching that Jesus was nothing more than human. He explained the title "Son of God" in terms of that moral-religious sonship that is the experience of all believers as they trust in God as their Father.[22] And he put the following statement in italics: *"The Gospel, as Jesus proclaimed it, has to do with the Father only, and not with the Son."*[23] At another point we read that Jesus "desired no other belief in his person and no other attachment to it than is contained in the keeping of his commandments."[24]

This does not mean, however, that Harnack viewed Jesus as unimportant to our Christian faith. Harnack stressed that Jesus is the

---

[20]Ibid., 63.

[21]Ibid., 159.

[22]Vos, in his *Self-disclosure of Jesus,* is especially helpful in criticizing "the theory of purely formal significance of the messianic consciousness" (chap. 7) and in expounding the various senses in which the title "Son of God" is used of Jesus in the four gospels (chaps. 10, 11, and 12).

[23]Harnack, *What Is Christianity?* 144.

[24]Ibid., 125.

Appointed of the Father and the Way to the Father. "It is not as a mere factor that he is connected with the Gospel," Harnack wrote, *"he was its personal realization and its strength, and this he is felt to be still."*[25]

It is impossible to appreciate the religious impact of liberalism upon so many in its generation unless it is understood that in liberalism Jesus was viewed not merely as the great Teacher, but also as the personal embodiment of the truth that he taught. As Harnack never tired of emphasizing, "Words effect nothing; it is the power of the personality that stands behind them."[26]

If Jesus is felt to be the personal realization and strength of the gospel "still" (see above), does that mean that Jesus still lives today? Well, Harnack would say, not if you mean that Jesus was actually raised from the grave. He made a sharp—and influential—distinction between the Easter *message* and the Easter *faith*. The Easter *message* was the message of the disciples about the empty grave and the post-resurrection appearances of Jesus. "But the Easter *faith*," he declared, "is the conviction that the crucified one gained a victory over death; that God is just and powerful; that he who is firstborn among many brethren still lives."[27]

The Easter faith is what really matters. "We must hold the Easter faith," Harnack argued, "even without the Easter message: 'Blessed are they that have not seen and yet have believed.'"[28] He continued: "Whatever may have happened at the grave and in the matter of the appearances, one thing is certain: *This grave was the birthplace of the indestructible belief that death is vanquished, that there is a life eternal."*[29]

---

[25]Ibid., 145 (Harnack's italics).

[26]Ibid., 48.

[27]Ibid., 161 (Harnack's italics).

[28]Ibid., 160.

[29]Ibid., 162 (Harnack's italics).

PART TWO:
SKEPTICISM REGARDING THE QUEST AND THE ASCENT OF RADICAL CRITICISM

4

The History-of-Religions School

Obviously, the changed outlook that we shall consider now in Part Two of our survey did not come about overnight. In hindsight, however, Harnack may be considered the end of an era in Gospels criticism—although he certainly was not viewed this way in his own time! Even before the publication of *What Is Christianity?* historians and New Testament scholars were beginning to see that the liberal Jesus could not really be drawn out of the sources (the gospel accounts), but was a product of the subjective liberal imagination. Many scholars played important roles in the transition from the liberalism that had reconstructed the life of Jesus with a large measure of confidence in the historical reliability of the Synoptic Gospels (particularly of Mark and Q) to the radicalism of Rudolf Bultmann, who was skeptical about our ability to know anything at all about the historical Jesus. We shall now consider just a few of the most important of those transitional figures. In some ways, of course, Reimarus and especially Strauss had earlier anticipated this development.

1. William Wrede (1859–1906)

In 1901 William Wrede, professor of New Testament at Breslau, published a most influential work, *Das Messiasgeheimnis in den*

59

Evangelien.[1] There Wrede argued that the Gospel of Mark, far from being the reliable account of the life of the historical Jesus that the liberals thought it was, was actually an elaborate theological interpretation devised (by the Marcan community, not by a single individual[2]) to bring the historical Jesus into line with the dogmatic Christ of the church's faith.

Wrede insisted that there is no reliable evidence that Jesus himself had ever claimed messiahship or acted as the Messiah. The earliest Christian believers recognized and accepted this fact. They preached that Jesus had *become* the Messiah, by God's appointment, by virtue of his resurrection. Remnants of this original Christology remain in the New Testament, Wrede argued, particularly in Acts 2:36—"Therefore let all Israel be assured of this: God has made this Jesus, whom you crucified, both Lord and Christ [Messiah]," having "raised this Jesus to life" (v. 32)—and in Romans 1:4—"who through the Spirit of holiness was declared with power to be the Son of God by his resurrection from the dead: Jesus Christ our Lord."

Soon, however, many Christians began to reflect on this, and they concluded that if Jesus was the Messiah *then,* then surely he must have been the Messiah during his earthly ministry—and surely he must have given clear evidence of his messiahship.

This new view was harmonized with the old one by the author of the Gospel of Mark (and by the believing community in which he lived) by introducing the idea of the messianic secret. Yes, Mark would have his readers believe, Jesus *was* indeed the Messiah before his resurrection, but this was made known to none except the demons and his own chosen disciples—and his disciples themselves did not really understand the secret until after the Resurrection.

In the Gospel of Mark, Jesus speaks in cryptic parables. Even his disciples do not understand. Why? Similarly, why does Jesus silence the demons who have a supernatural knowledge of his identity (1:24–25, 34; 3:11–12; 5:7)? Why does he command that no one be told about certain miraculous healings (1:44; 5:43; 7:36; 8:26)? Why does he

---

[1] This radically trend-setting work was not translated into English until 1971: William Wrede, *The Messianic Secret*, trans. J. C. G. Greig (Cambridge: James Clarke, 1971).

[2] Wrede, *Messianic Secret*, 145.

warn the disciples after Peter's confession of him as the Messiah not to tell anyone who he is (8:30)? And after his transfiguration, why does he tell his disciples not to tell anyone what they have seen (9:9)? What we must see, according to Wrede, is that Jesus never said these things. These accounts are Mark's literary devices to explain the puzzling lack of historical evidence that Jesus ever claimed to be the Messiah! The messianic secret forms "a theological bridge constructed by the Christian community from the non-messianic life of Jesus to the Church's messianic understanding of that life."[3] (According to Wrede, Matthew and Luke made use of Mark's Gospel, but they did not retain Mark's theory of the "messianic secret.")

Wrede's theory has been considered truly groundbreaking, and it "has remained determinative for New Testament work right up to the present."[4] For example, Rudolf Bultmann, the major twentieth-century figure in Gospels criticism, praises Wrede highly and presupposes Wrede's theory in his own work. In place of the liberalism that presented *Jesus* as the creative force in Christianity, and the synoptics (especially Mark) as reliable guides to Jesus' history, Wrede presented the early *church*—not only the apostle Paul, but also the author of Mark and the other Evangelists[5]—as the true originators of the Christian faith, and all four gospels (not just John) as thoroughly theological works presenting a thoroughly divine (as well as thoroughly human) Jesus Christ.

For orthodox, Bible-believing Christians, the radical approach to the gospel texts is certainly no better theologically than the liberal approach, since the radical, fully as much as the liberal, immediately excludes all references to the supernatural from the realm of history. However, the radical interpretation is often much stronger *exegetically.* That is, the radical recognizes that a supernatural Christ is presented in the gospel texts, even though he is convinced that a modern person cannot believe that the incarnate Son of God actually appeared in history. For example, in contrast to the liberal insistence on the simplic-

---

[3]Grieg in his preface to Wrede, *Messianic Secret,* x.

[4]Ibid., ix.

[5]The term often used by New Testament scholars to refer to the authors of the four gospels.

ity of Mark's Gospel and the merely human Jesus presented there, Bultmann emphasizes that

> Mark in his own way also [compared with Matthew] brings to view that fact that eschatological salvation became history. . . . Chief emphasis falls upon the miracles and miraculous events like the baptism and the transfiguration. In these the true nature of the Son of God . . . appears. . . . Jesus' life is not an episode of world history but the miraculous manifestation of divine dealing in the cloak of earthly occurrence. By including the debates of Jesus along with the miracles Jesus is presented less than in Matthew as teacher of the Church and more as the Son of God, who unmasks the anti-godliness of Jewish tradition.[6]

While not necessarily agreeing with every statement even there (what is the meaning of "not an episode of world history"?), the Christian can surely learn much from the insights of such a radical as Bultmann concerning the true force of the Marcan account and the true nature of the Marcan Jesus (a Jesus in whom Bultmann finds it impossible to believe[7]). What such radical exegesis brings out clearly is the fact that the so-called historical Jesus—a merely human, nonsupernatural Jesus—is a hypothesis of modern Gospels criticism working on post-Enlightenment, naturalistic presuppositions—and certainly cannot be discovered from the gospel accounts themselves. Thus, when one reads that Wrede's "book signaled the defeat of the conception of the Gospel as a historical presentation of the life of Jesus,"[8] one must keep clearly in mind that "historical" in that statement means by definition "nonsupernatural"—that which is in accord with the closed continuum of ongoing, analogous human experience.

In his emphasis on the theological purposes of each Evangelist

---

[6]Rudolf Bultmann, *Theology of the New Testament,* 2 vols., trans. Kendrick Grobel (New York: Charles Scribner's Sons, 1955), 2:125.

[7]Ben F. Meyer states well the inevitable clash between a post-Enlightenment worldview and the Christian faith: "The heritage of Christian belief affirms as indispensable what the heritage of modern culture excludes as impossible" (*The Aims of Jesus* [London: SCM, 1979], 15).

[8]Ibid., 47.

and on the literary devices used by each to accomplish his purposes, Wrede may accurately be said to have initiated the critical methodologies that later came to be known as form criticism and redaction criticism.

A theory as influential as Wrede's demands some response even in a survey as brief as this. For many of his critics, the fundamental flaw in his reconstruction appears immediately in his hypothesis of an original Christology in which Jesus was viewed as becoming the Messiah at his resurrection. Does Wrede substantiate that this was the primitive Christian belief? Does the Resurrection itself adequately account for it?

Both Schweitzer and Sanday in their early responses challenged Wrede at this point. Schweitzer noted that some in Jesus' day believed that John the Baptist had been raised from the dead (Mark 6:14–16), but they did not for that reason declare John to be the Messiah.[9] And Sanday wrote: "It is true enough that the belief in the Resurrection bore a great weight of superstructure in apostolic times. But [in Wrede's theory] . . . it is not only the foundation stone, but apparently the sole foundation of the whole edifice of Christianity. Does Wrede really believe this?"[10]

Sanday appealed to the following passage from *Jesus,* by Wilhelm Bousset:

> We have certain knowledge that the belief existed from the very beginning among the Christian community that Jesus was Messiah, and, arguing backwards, we can assert that the rise of such a belief would be absolutely inexplicable if Jesus had not declared to His disciples in His lifetime that He was the Messiah. It is quite conceivable that the first disciples of Jesus, who by His death and burial had seen all their hopes shattered and their belief in His Messiahship destroyed, might have *returned* to that belief under the influence of their resurrection experiences, if they had formerly possessed it on the ground of the utterances and general conduct of Jesus. But it would

---

[9]Albert Schweitzer, *The Quest of the Historical Jesus,* trans. W. Montgomery, 2d ed. (1911; reprint, London: Adam & Charles Black, 1945), 343.

[10]William Sanday, *The Life of Christ in Recent Research* (New York: Oxford University Press, 1907), 75.

be wholly incomprehensible that the belief should have *originated* in their hearts after the catastrophe.[11]

When the antisupernaturalist Wrede recognized the pervasively supernatural figure of Christ in Mark—and that both his death and his resurrection were elements in his distinctively messianic work—he was forced to conclude that the entire narrative is essentially unhistorical. Thus, there was in Wrede a much more thoroughgoing repudiation of the gospel tradition than in Ritschlian liberalism. And having radically cut the cord attaching the messianic faith of the primitive Christian community to the life and teaching of Jesus himself, Wrede could offer no clear and adequate explanation for the origin of that faith.

As we noted earlier, Wrede placed great weight on Acts 2:36 as evidence for the supposedly original Christology of the church. He boldly affirmed, "This saying quite by itself would prove that there was in primitive Christianity a view in accordance with which Jesus was not the messiah in his earthly life."[12]

On a cursory reading, it can appear that Peter is indeed teaching in that text that Jesus' messiahship began at his resurrection. But a more careful reading of the context makes it clear that Peter is here speaking of Jesus' exaltation, of the fact that the risen Savior entered upon a new stage of his lordship and messiahship that transcended the earlier stage. Read the whole of Peter's sermon, beginning back at verse 14. And go on to read Peter's next discourse, Acts 3:13–26, in which he explains more fully what has happened. God "has glorified his servant Jesus" (v. 13). The glorification of the Servant of God was the prophet Isaiah's message, and the title Servant (*pais* in the Greek of the Septuagint and of Acts 3:13) has clearly messianic connotations. "You disowned the Holy and Righteous One" (v. 14), who already stood in relation to God as the Messiah. "You killed the author of life"

---

[11]W. Bousset, *Jesus* (New York: Putnam's Sons, 1906), 168–69. Tuckett cites not only Bousset, but also Jülicher, Peake, Rawlinson, and Taylor as presenting this same argument. Christopher Tuckett, ed., *The Messianic Secret* (Philadelphia: Fortress, 1983), 23. As noted later in this chapter, the book *Jesus* represents an earlier view, not the final stage, in Bousset's thinking.

[12]Wrede, *Messianic Secret,* 216.

(v. 15). "But this is how God fulfilled what he had foretold through all the prophets, saying that *his Christ* [his Messiah] would suffer" (v. 18, emphasis added). Peter's clear statement here should remove all doubt as to whether he and the earliest church considered Jesus to have been the Messiah in his earthly life prior to the Resurrection.

When we move to a consideration of the data in Mark's Gospel that Wrede presented as evidence for his theory of the messianic secret, we may begin by asking why these phenomena are not "explicable as simple historic fact, rather than as the church's later dogmatic superimposition on the tradition."[13] One answer Wrede gave to that question is that he could find in Mark only the Christian conception of the Messiah and not the contemporary Jewish conception. Schweitzer and Bowman ask what would seem to be the natural question here:

> Why may this not represent historic fact and the mind of Jesus? May it not be that the real *secret* related to the *kind* of Messiah Jesus was— one who should suffer in order to save . . . and that it was this which presented itself as the "stumbling-block" to his contemporary's recognition of him?[14]

In criticism since Wrede, it has become almost a cliché to insist that the Gospels are not "biographies," but "kerygma" (a term taken from the Greek and meaning "proclamation, preaching")—written with the single purpose of bringing forth and strengthening faith in Jesus Christ. There is an important insight in that view, as we shall note later. Martin Hengel is surely correct in saying that *"Mark only reports history which has undergone the deliberate reflection of faith."* He is also correct, however, when he observes that "the fatal error in the interpretation of the Gospels in general and of Mark in particular has been that scholars have thought that they had to decide between preaching and historical narration, that here there could only be an either-or." Why should we think that Mark faced such a choice? After

---

[13]John Wick Bowman, "Messianic Secret," in *Twentieth Century Encyclopedia of Religious Knowledge,* ed. Lefferts A. Loetscher, 2 vols. (Grand Rapids: Baker, 1955), 2:731.

[14]Ibid. Cf. Schweitzer, *Quest of the Historical Jesus,* 336ff.

all, in his Bible Mark was given "the model of Old Testament historiography . . . where this unity of narration and proclamation is often visible."[15]

The reader who begins with Wrede's book and then reads the Gospel of Mark itself will be struck by the fact that the so-called secrecy phenomena are not nearly as unified and consistent as Wrede supposes. This is crucial, because the plausibility of Wrede's theory rests on its alleged ability to reveal a uniform pattern in Mark's Gospel. Without that, the theory falls apart.

Those who wish to examine the evidence at length should consult the chapters by James D. G. Dunn and by Heikki Räisänen in the volume of essays entitled *The Messianic Secret,* edited by Christopher Tuckett and noted above. What the data do show is that Jesus was characterized by reserve and passivity in this matter of the disclosure of his messiahship. The "servant song" recorded by Isaiah and appealed to by Matthew also describes the Jesus who moves through the pages of Mark's Gospel: "He will not quarrel or cry out; no one will hear his voice in the streets" (Matt. 12:19). What Wrede cites as marks of "the secrecy dogma" are often simply evidences of Jesus' God-centered messiahship. In the carrying out of his messianic role, Jesus is totally in submission to God's plan and God's time.

With regard to the many references to demon possession in Mark, commands to keep silent are not found in the account of the daughter of the Syrophoenician woman (7:24–30), nor in the case of the boy brought to Jesus after the Transfiguration (9:14–29). The Gerasene demoniac is expressly commanded to go home to his family "and tell them how much the Lord has done for you." The man obeyed that command, "and all the people were amazed" (5:19–20). Mark 1:34, like 1:25 and 3:12, does record that Jesus "would not let the demons speak because they knew who he was," but does that present a problem

---

[15]Martin Hengel, "Literary, Theological, and Historical Problems in the Gospel of Mark," *The Gospel and the Gospels,* ed. Peter Stuhlmacher (Grand Rapids: Eerdmans, 1991), 219, 224 (Hengel's italics). See Meredith G. Kline's helpful study, "The Old Testament Origins of the Gospel Genre," in *The Westminster Theological Journal* 38 (Fall 1975):1–27.

of "secrecy" for us?[16] Note that it was the demons who were forbidden to speak, not the persons out of whom the demons were cast. Those who received the Messiah's mercy were not charged to tell no one about it. Is there not an evident incongruity in permitting the agents of Satan to be the heralds of the Lord's Christ? (Remember the false charge recorded in Mark 3:22.) Hengel comments, "At the same time Mark wants . . . to demonstrate the contrast between the people and the disciples, who do not yet know Jesus' status, and the invisible world of the spirits, who from the beginning have recognized Jesus as their messianic conqueror."[17]

People who were healed were usually encouraged to disclose their healings and testify to the messianic Son of Man's mercy and power. There are, however, four exceptions to that pattern: the leper in Mark 1:40–45 is commanded not to tell anyone; those who witnessed the raising of Jairus's daughter were given "strict orders not to let anyone know about this" (5:43); there is a similar command in 7:36; and the blind man healed at Bethsaida was told not to go into the village (8:26).

An explanation for these commands is not always given in the account. The negative command to the leper is coupled with the positive command to show himself to the priest in order to fulfill the Mosaic law's requirements for ceremonial cleansing "as a testimony to them" (1:44)—which hardly seems to be in the interests of keeping the matter a secret! And notice that verse 45 is an example of what, as a matter of fact, so frequently happened: the command to keep quiet was ignored and the news was spread! How does that fit Mark's alleged purpose of explaining why it was that Jesus was not known to be the Messiah during his lifetime? The prohibition by itself would not have had that result if the prohibition was not obeyed!

And Mark 1:45 reveals why Jesus so often desired to keep his presence and activity quiet: "Instead he went out and began to talk freely, spreading the news. As a result, Jesus could no longer enter a

---

[16]Any reference to demonic activity, of course, is immediately marked out by Wrede as unhistorical. He *has* to seek a rational explanation for the presence in Mark's account for passages like 1:23–26.

[17]Hengel, "Literary, Theological, and Historical Problems," 226.

town openly but stayed outside in lonely places. Yet the people still came to him from everywhere."

A certain reserve was necessary for the performing of God's mission in God's way and in God's time. Jesus was not a "miracle worker" in the sense the world too often sees on display—the religious showman! Jesus' miracles were integrated with and subordinated to his overall redemptive purpose.

It is simply not possible for us today to determine why in some cases Jesus took steps to ensure secrecy (see 1:37), when in other cases he did not. Some miracles were performed quite openly in the public marketplaces (6:56). Sometimes there were even mass healings (1:32). Returning to the point made earlier, that the Marcan data do not present the homogenous pattern required to support Wrede's theory, Vos writes, "Had the writer been guided by the fixed idea that the messianic secrecy must always accompany the messianic miracles, then he also would not have failed to introduce the idea of secrecy uniformly and consistently."[18]

With regard to Jesus' teaching in parables (note in particular 4:10–12, where the reason for such a teaching form is given), emphasis is placed on the revelation, the disclosure, that is brought in this way— "The secret of the kingdom of God has been given to you"—while at the same time there is a purposeful drawing of the line between those who are given understanding and those who are not. Schweitzer later recognized in this—and in such a saying as "For many are invited, but few are chosen" (Matt. 22:14)—evidence of the predestinarianism so characteristic of Jesus' theology, but so offensive to Schweitzer.

Finally, it should be noted that Wrede had to acknowledge that Mark's Gospel contains certain "contradictions" (Wrede's term) of the messianic secrecy pattern (if we can still speak of a "pattern" after we have examined the data in Mark!): Peter's confession of Jesus as the Christ (8:29), the shouts of the people as Jesus enters Jerusalem, proclaiming him to be the Messiah of Psalm 118 (11:9–10), and Jesus' confession before the high priest (14:61–64).[19] And to Wrede's list we

---

[18]Geerhardus Vos, *The Self-disclosure of Jesus,* ed. Johannes G. Vos (Grand Rapids: Eerdmans, 1954), 72.

[19]Wrede, *Messianic Secret,* 124–29.

could surely add the testimony of the Father from heaven as the Spirit descended on Jesus at his baptism (1:11), the charge brought against Jesus to Pilate (15:26), and the mocking words of the chief priests and the teachers of the law standing before the cross: "Let this Christ, this King of Israel, come down now from the cross, that we may see and believe" (15:32)—none of which accords with the theory that Mark was trying to convey the notion that Jesus' messiahship was a "secret" before his resurrection.

Wrede's solution to the apparent problem for his theory was twofold. His first suggestion was this:

> The most obvious idea is that the evangelist has taken over traditional materials in which the idea of the secret messiahship was not present, and a few points do in fact admit of explanation in this way. For example, this explanation is easily sustained in regard to the entry into Jerusalem.

Wrede quickly added, however, that this explanation is "by no means adequate, but a second and . . . a more important approach is open to us." This second approach is to stress that Mark was faced with an inevitable tension between his two conflicting purposes. On the one hand, he wanted to account for the disciples' failure to recognize Jesus as the Messiah before the Resurrection. But, on the other hand, Mark wanted to present Jesus as one who was already the Messiah and thus lived "a life full of messianic manifestations." Thus, "it is not hard to see that the idea of the messianic secret was not simply *capable* of introducing contradictions by chance, but that it was almost *bound* of necessity to evoke such."[20]

Despite Wrede's efforts to explain the appearance of such contradictions to his theory, these passages remained for him essentially unassimilated data. If Mark was the subtle literary craftsman Wrede emphasizes him to be, why was his messianic secrecy scheme so inconsistently carried out?

According to Wrede's theory, Mark viewed the disciples as blind to Jesus' messiahship until the Resurrection. Thus, Mark presented his readers with a sharp contrast between messianic secrecy and ignorance

---

[20]Ibid., 125–26 (Wrede's italics).

before the Resurrection and joyful acknowledgment afterward. The thesis of ignorance on the part of the disciples before the Resurrection is not tenable, however. Yes, there is much evidence of bewilderment and amazement on the part of the disciples in Mark's Gospel. If those references are isolated from their context, Wrede's view might seem plausible. Mark, however, also emphasizes the faith, apprehension, commitment, and loyalty of the disciples. *Both* elements are part of his record.

Consider, for example, the confession of Peter at Caesarea Philippi (Mark 8:27–30). Wrede is correct in saying that earlier critics had misunderstood this scene when they viewed it as marking a great turning point in the ministry of Jesus and his disciples.[21] But Wrede himself cannot do justice to the strong emphasis here on the understanding and faith of Peter.

Mark is not highlighting a *new* understanding on the part of Peter and the other disciples here. Wrede is correct on that. But Mark is highlighting their true understanding. Jesus' question is "What is *your* estimate of my person and work?"—compared with the false estimates of others—not "what is your *new* estimate?" This question is not asked here in the context of a mighty miracle or some new divine revelation. Jesus is simply eliciting from the disciples what he regards as a true estimate of himself—that he is the Messiah—as preparation for teaching them about his upcoming suffering, death, and resurrection (8:31). The newness lies in that teaching by Jesus, not in the confession by Peter.

With Peter's faith there is immediately joined an element of misunderstanding and amazement, a lack of thorough understanding of the Messiah's work (8:32–33). This shows that there has not just been a great turning point in the disciples' understanding. They are not now entering a period of full faith, unclouded by doubts. But Mark does present the disciples as men of faith—specifically, faith in Jesus as the Messiah. They do not come to regard him as the Messiah for the first time after his resurrection. Rather, at that time they come to understand with new clarity the full implications of his messianic person and mission.

---

[21]Ibid., 115ff.

2. Wilhelm Bousset (1865–1920)

Although William Wrede has had a more lasting influence, the second New Testament professor[22] whom we shall consider in this chapter (much more briefly) was a more typical representative of the history-of-religions school of New Testament criticism. Neill writes:

> In my judgment, one man stands far above all others as a contributor to the development of this religio-historical school of interpretation, which sees the New Testament as one part of a much wider historical phenomenon, the religion of the Levant in the period before and after Jesus Christ. Wilhelm Bousset . . .[23]

Bousset is now viewed as a transitional figure in the history of Gospels criticism, and he himself passed through three stages in the development of his own thinking. In an early book (1902),[24] Bousset presented a rather naive liberalism, stressing Jesus' originality and rejecting all eschatological "accretions" in the Gospels.

In a later book,[25] Bousset continued to present an essentially liberal position, but he modified his views in two important ways that moved him in the direction of radicalism. First, he now recognized the eschatological element in Jesus' own messianic consciousness. Jesus did think of himself as the Danielic Son of Man. Indeed, that was the only messianic title "which Jesus certainly applied to himself." This title included the ideas of preexistence and future judgeship over all the nations, but it is "inconceivable" that Jesus believed this concerning himself. And yet to sustain himself in his closing days of despair, Jesus did grasp onto the idea of a future coming in glory. Thus, the title was

---

[22]First at Göttingen and later at Giessen.

[23]Stephen Neill and Tom Wright, *The Interpretation of the New Testament 1861–1986* (Oxford: Oxford University Press, 1988), 175. The original designation of this critical school is one of those delightful German compounds, *die religionsgeschichtliche Schule*.

[24]Wilhelm Bousset, *Jesu Predigt in ihrem Gegensatz zum Judentum* [Jesus' preaching in its contrast to Judaism] (Göttingen: Vandenhoeck & Ruprecht, 1892; text-fiche, Chicago: American Theological Library Association, 1985).

[25]W. Bousset, *Jesus,* trans. Janet Penrose Trevelyan (New York: G. P. Putnam's Sons, 1906).

not adopted by Jesus "until the end of his life" and was not well suited to Jesus' essential teaching.[26] Second, with regard to the question of how much in the gospel accounts goes back to Jesus himself and how much owes its origin to the early church, Bousset took a much more radical position than that taken by the liberal Harnack just a few years earlier.

By the time he wrote his most famous and widely discussed book, *Kyrios Christos* (1913),[27] Bousset, along with Hermann Gunkel, his colleague on the Giessen faculty, had begun to apply the *religionsgeschichtliche Methode* to the Bible. He now admitted the full, supernatural significance of the title Son of Man, but he no longer ascribed that title to Jesus. It was now explained as the product of Palestinian Christianity, and the title Lord *(kyrios)* was seen as the product of Hellenistic Christianity. Bousset's emphasis now fell on the Christian community as the creative force (the radical emphasis), rather than on the creative force of Jesus, his personality, life, and teaching (the liberal emphasis). In the Jerusalem church, Bousset insisted, Jesus was viewed as the coming Son of Man, but was not viewed as Lord; he was not the object of faith. It was the Antioch church, and most importantly the apostle Paul, who first applied the title *kyrios,* so popular in the pagan religious cults, to Jesus.

In Bousset's reconstruction of early church history, there is a certain formal similarity to F. C. Baur. Baur had assigned the New Testament books to various chronological periods on the basis of the *Tendenz* discerned in them. Bousset assigned the various elements in the gospel tradition to various geographical and cultural areas in the first century, and on his radical presuppositions very little was assigned to Jesus himself.

Earlier I mentioned that J. Gresham Machen had studied under the Ritschlian liberal, Wilhelm Herrmann. Machen also studied under Bousset, and in one of his finest scholarly works he delivered a masterful critique of Bousset's principal thesis.[28] Machen examined evi-

---

[26]Ibid., 183, 203, 193.

[27]Wilhelm Bousset, *Kyrios Christos,* trans. John E. Steely (Nashville: Abingdon, 1970).

[28]J. Gresham Machen, *The Origin of Paul's Religion* (New York: Macmillan, 1921; Grand Rapids: Eerdmans, 1947), especially chap. 8. In this same book, Machen

dence from Paul's own letters for the Palestinian origin of the title *Lord* for Jesus (in particular, Gal. 1:19 and 1 Cor. 16:22). Machen agreed that the title was popular in paganism (think of 1 Cor. 8:5–6), but he noted that that fact does not establish that the apostle Paul took up the title from that source. Any Christian missionary has to use language understandable to his hearers, and if Paul had sought a term to designate Jesus as divine and yet distinct from God the Father, the word at hand was indeed *kyrios*. But, of course, there was an additional and vitally significant reason for Paul's use of that title, the Septuagint background. Not only the Jews, but also the Gentile proselytes, had the Septuagint (the Greek translation of the Old Testament) as their Bible. The theological implications of this title, used in the Septuagint as the covenant name of God (the Greek translation for the tetragrammaton, *Yahweh*), would be immediately clear to them. And keep in mind what Bousset seemed to overlook, that Paul himself was not a Hellenist in religious background, but a Jew, a Pharisee. Schweitzer compares "those who labor to explain" Paul "on the basis of Hellenism" to "a man who should bring water from a long distance in leaky watering-cans in order to water a garden lying beside a stream."[29]

---

analyzes Wrede's *Paulus* (Halle: Gebauer-Schwetschke, 1904), translated into English by Edward Lummis as *Paul* (London: P. Green, 1907). For a study of the meaning of the title *kyrios* as used of Jesus in the Gospels, see Vos, *Self-disclosure of Jesus,* chap. 9.

[29]Albert Schweitzer, *The Mysticism of Paul the Apostle,* trans. William Montgomery, 2d ed. (London: Adam and Charles Black, 1953), 140.

5

Thoroughgoing Eschatology

T$_{HE}$ "$_{THOROUGHGOING\ ESCHATOLOGY}$" of Albert Schweitzer[1] has much in common with the approach discussed in the previous chapter. This is shown by the fact that the two scholars whom we shall now cite as providing preparatory development for Schweitzer's approach are usually categorized as important members of the history-of-religions school.

1. Preparatory Development

In a brief treatise published in 1888,[2] Wilhelm Baldensperger (1856–1936)[3] argued that as long as we think only in terms of legalistic Pharisaism, we will not understand first-century Judaism in all its richness, which included supernatural (versus merely political) eschatological hopes and piety. Baldensperger declared that Jesus of

---

[1]Schweitzer's own term was *konsequente Eschatologie.*

[2]Wilhelm Baldensperger, *Das Selbstbewusstsein Jesu im Lichte der messianischen Hoffnungen seiner Zeit* [The Self-consciousness of Jesus in the Light of the Messianic Hopes of His Time] (Strassburg: J. H. E. Heitz, 1888).

[3]When he wrote this treatise, Baldensperger was a pastor in Alsace. Later he became professor of New Testament, first at Giessen and then at Strassburg.

Nazareth had such a fully developed eschatology, which displayed many points of contact with so-called late Jewish thought as represented in such apocalyptic literature as *The Similitudes of Enoch* and *Fourth Esdras*. Baldensperger himself, however, did not draw the conclusions from this basic thesis that Schweitzer was later to draw. Instead, he insisted that the deepest motives of the messianic ministry of Jesus were religio-ethical, and thus he did not allow his new studies in Jewish eschatology to radically alter his basically liberal picture of Jesus.

In 1892 Johannes Weiss (1863–1914)[4] published a brief treatise that had an even greater influence on Schweitzer.[5] In sharp distinction from the central teaching of Ritschlian liberalism, Weiss maintained that the kingdom of God that Jesus preached was God-centered, transcendental, wholly future (but very near at hand), and to be brought in solely by God's activity. According to Weiss, Jesus expected that the people of God would have to repent of their sins as preparation for the kingdom that God would establish. When the people did not repent, Jesus accepted the necessity of his own death as a vicarious repentance on their behalf, thus opening the way for God to bring in the kingdom:

> Jesus concluded that the establishment by God of the messianic Kingdom could not yet take place; that an enormous obstacle, the guilt of the people, had to be removed; and that he would not live to see this happen, but first must fall victim to the hatred of his opponents. But from Jesus' religious understanding of his whole life, this could not mean the failure of his work. It must rather be a means for bringing about the final goal. And since the sin which will cause his death is at the same time the chief obstacle to the coming of the Kingdom, he seized upon the audacious and paradoxical idea—or the idea seized him—that his death itself should be the ransom for the people otherwise destined to destruction (Mark 10:45). He must give

---

[4]Professor of New Testament at Göttingen, later at Marburg, and finally at Heidelberg. He was the son of Bernhard Weiss, a New Testament professor often characterized as a "conservative liberal," and the son-in-law of Albrecht Ritschl.

[5]Johannes Weiss, *Die Predigt Jesu vom Reiche Gottes,* 3d ed. (Göttingen: Vandenhoeck & Ruprecht, 1964); *Jesus' Proclamation of the Kingdom of God,* trans. and ed. Richard Hyde Hiers and David Darrimore Holland (Philadelphia: Fortress, 1971).

up his life *huper pollon* as a *lutron,* which the many, the people themselves, could not offer.[6]

The ethical teaching of Jesus, according to Weiss, should not be thought of as presenting the ethics of the kingdom, but rather as setting forth the penitential discipline required of those who would enter the kingdom of God. Thus, it may be referred to as an *Interimsethik,* an ethic for the interim remaining before the manifestation of the kingdom.[7]

Weiss limited his application of the eschatological emphasis to this one subject of the kingdom. (And, in a revised edition published in 1900, he modified his position so considerably that he was no longer so consistently eschatological even on that subject.[8]) But Weiss had planted the seeds that were soon brought to full bloom by Albert Schweitzer.

2. Albert Schweitzer (1875–1965)

Albert Schweitzer was a truly amazing man. It is difficult for students today to fully appreciate how widespread his fame was during his lifetime and how highly he was esteemed. In the last decades of his life,

---

[6]Weiss, *Jesus' Proclamation,* 87–88.

[7]Ibid., 105–14. Again, the sharp contrast with Ritschlianism is evident. As Ben F. Meyer reminds us: "The centre of gravity in liberal theology was a timeless ethic . . . never better expressed than in the Sermon on the Mount and the parables" (*The Aims of Jesus* [London: SCM, 1979], 39).

[8]For a comparison of the two editions, and a discussion of Weiss's personal theology (entitled "Ritschlian Theology, Nevertheless"!), see the "Introduction by the Editors" in Weiss, *Jesus' Proclamation,* 16–24, 49–53. At Marburg, Rudolf Bultmann studied New Testament under Johannes Weiss and systematic theology under Julius Kaftan. In the foreword to this English translation of Weiss (p. xi), Bultmann quotes Kaftan's classroom statement: "If the Kingdom of God is an eschatological matter, then it is a useless concept so far as dogmatics is concerned." Since Weiss shared the same naturalistic presuppositions as Kaftan, he agreed with that statement. At least he agreed that Jesus' concept of the kingdom is theologically of no use unless significantly reinterpreted— along liberal lines. What Weiss strove to make clear, in the interests of honest historical scholarship, was the sharp difference between Jesus' teaching and Ritschl's. He also made clear that his personal religious preference was for the latter.

many regarded Schweitzer as the leading citizen of the world! In 1952 he was awarded the Nobel Peace Prize. Americans in particular were fascinated by his self-sacrificing service in Africa, his example of humanitarianism in action, and his ethical mysticism often summed up in the phrase "a reverence for life"—for all life, down to its most primitive forms (a principle that made Schweitzer notorious for his refusal to kill even a mosquito or other disease-carrying insect). However, all his ethics, all his mysticism, and all his medical missionary service were totally divorced, as we shall see, from the historic Christian faith.

Born in Alsace-Lorraine, Schweitzer was from birth a man with two countries.[9] The eldest son of a Lutheran minister, he first studied theology (under H. J. Holtzmann[10]) and philosophy (under Wilhelm Windelband[11]) at Strassburg, receiving his doctor's degree in philosophy in 1899 with a thesis on "Kant's Philosophy of Religion" and his doctor's degree in theology in 1900. During these years he also studied music, and became a recognized expert on Johann Sebastian Bach, organ technique, and organ building, publishing a biography of Bach in 1905 and a treatise on organ building in 1906. The book of particular interest to us here, *Von Reimarus zu Wrede* [From Reimarus to Wrede], was also published in 1906.[12]

In 1913 Schweitzer received a doctor's degree in medicine with a dissertation on "The Psychiatric Estimate of Jesus," a defense of the sanity of Jesus of Nazareth (and after we have considered the thinking of the historical Jesus according to Schweitzer, you will understand why Schweitzer might well have felt that such a defense was necessary!). Immediately upon receiving his degree in medicine, Schweitzer

---

[9]The Alsace-Lorraine region on the border of France and Germany was under German control from 1871 until the end of World War I (1919) and again during World War II (1939–1945). Between the wars, and after 1945, it has been a part of France.

[10]See chap. 3, sec. 1, above.

[11]Windelband's much-praised textbook, *Geschichte der Philosophie,* was published in Freiburg by J. C. B. Mohr in 1892 and translated into English as *A History of Philosophy* by James H. Tufts (New York: Macmillan, 1893). A reprint paperback edition was published in two volumes by Harper in 1958.

[12]English translation, *The Quest of the Historical Jesus,* trans. W. Montgomery, 2d ed. (1911; reprint, London: Adam and Charles Black, 1945).

and his wife, who had trained as a nurse, moved to Lambarene in the Gabon province of French Equatorial Africa to establish a hospital under the auspices of a French missionary society in order to help atone, as Schweitzer put it, for the great injustices whites had done to black peoples over the centuries. Except for the interruptions caused by the two world wars (he was imprisoned first by the Germans and then by the French during World War I), and by occasional organ recitals and lecture tours throughout Europe to raise money for his hospital, Schweitzer continued to work in his hospital in Africa for the last forty-two years of his life.[13]

In *The Quest of the Historical Jesus,* Schweitzer presented a devastating critique of the various previous attempts to discover the Jesus of history. Schweitzer concluded that in seeking the "real" Jesus, the Jesus not draped in the clothing of the orthodox Christology, New Testament scholars had ended up constructing a totally unhistorical Jesus, a Jesus to fit their own philosophical and religious prejudices. They had found a Jesus who looked more like a deist, a follower of Hegel, or a Protestant liberal than the actual Jesus of history.[14] Schweitzer wrote:

> The Jesus of Nazareth who came forward publicly as the Messiah, who preached the ethic of the Kingdom of God, who founded the Kingdom of Heaven upon earth, and died to give His work its final consecration, never had existence. He is a figure designed by rationalism, endowed with life by liberalism, and clothed by modern theology in an historical garb.[15]

Schweitzer insisted that the whole methodology of trying to distinguish between what is "kernel" and what is "husk" in the synoptic accounts was on the wrong track:[16]

> We may take all that is reported as either historical or unhistorical, but, in respect of the definite predictions of the passion, death, and

---

[13]See his interesting autobiography, *Out of My Life and Thought,* trans. C. T. Campion (New York: New American Library, 1949).

[14]William M. Thompson, *The Jesus Debate* (New York: Paulist, 1985), 93.

[15]Schweitzer, *Quest of the Historical Jesus,* 396.

[16]Remember the discussion of Harnack in chap. 3, sec. 3, above.

resurrection, we ought to give up taking the reference to the passion as historical and letting the rest go; we may accept the idea of the atoning death, or we may reject it, but we ought not to ascribe to Jesus a feeble, an anaemic version of this idea, while setting down to the account of the Pauline theology the interpretation of the passion which we actually find in Mark.[17]

Paradoxically, however, as many have noted, Schweitzer himself "proceeded to erect a life of Jesus of his own, using primarily the same technique"![18] Jeremias speaks of the "real tragedy that Albert Schweitzer . . . should himself have been ensnared by the fallacy of psychological reconstruction."[19]

In presenting his own analysis of the synoptic record, Schweitzer acknowledged that he had learned much from Wrede.[20] What Wrede described as being Mark's dogma, however, Schweitzer insisted was Jesus' dogma![21] The so-called secrecy phenomena in Mark's Gospel were historical and point to Jesus' secret, namely, that he was to be the future King and Judge, the Son of Man who would come from heaven. Indeed, that secret, that faith, dominated Jesus' thinking and caused him to view everything in terms of eschatology, in terms of the coming age when the prospective Messiah would be revealed as the actual Messiah.[22]

Schweitzer agreed with Wrede that there is much confusion and apparent self-contradiction in Mark's account. Schweitzer insisted,

---

[17]Schweitzer, *Quest of the Historical Jesus,* 331.

[18]Charles C. Anderson, *Critical Quests of Jesus* (Grand Rapids: Eerdmans, 1969), 18.

[19]Joachim Jeremias, *The Problem of the Historical Jesus* (Philadelphia: Fortress, 1972), 6. David Cairns writes: "Ironically, Schweitzer himself unconsciously proved himself to be the last of the First Questers, since he offered his own interpretation of Jesus somewhat along the same lines as his predecessors, although his picture was startlingly unlike theirs" ("The Motives and Scope of Historical Inquiry about Jesus," *Scottish Journal of Theology* 29 [1976]: 337).

[20]Review chap. 4, sec. 1, above.

[21]Schweitzer contrasts Wrede's view and his own as the difference between "thoroughgoing scepticism" (Wrede) and "thoroughgoing eschatology" (Schweitzer). See his *Quest of the Historical Jesus,* chap. 19.

[22]Vos calls Schweitzer's position "the theory of prospective Messiahship" (*The Self-disclosure of Jesus,* ed. Johannes G. Vos [Grand Rapids: Eerdmans, 1954], chap. 5).

however, that "the chaotic confusion of the narratives ought to have suggested . . . that the events had been thrown into this confusion by the volcanic force of an incalculable personality, not by some kind of carelessness or freak of the tradition."[23] He also explained,

> There is, on the one hand, the eschatological solution [Schweitzer's], which at one stroke raises the Marcan account as it stands, with all its disconnectedness and inconsistencies, into genuine history; and there is, on the other hand, the literary solution [Wrede's], which regards the incongruous dogmatic element as interpolated by the earliest Evangelist into the tradition and therefore strikes out the Messianic claim altogether from the historical life of Jesus. *Tertium non datur.*[24]

According to Schweitzer, Mark's presentation, including the "secrecy phenomena," is historical. The key to understanding the account is to see that Jesus did not view himself as the Messiah already, but as the Messiah-designate. At first, this secret belonged to Jesus only. At the Transfiguration, it was revealed to the three most intimate disciples.[25] At Caesarea Philippi, Peter disclosed it to the other disciples.[26] Then Judas betrayed the secret to the high priest, who made it known to the mob, with the result that Jesus was put to death for his messianic claim.

Schweitzer emphasized, however, that Jesus was not content simply to move through his ministry passively, letting history take its

---

[23]Schweitzer, *Quest of the Historical Jesus,* 349. Notice that Schweitzer's emphasis on "the volcanic force" of Jesus' "incalculable personality" is the liberal emphasis as over against the radical emphasis (for example, Wrede's) on the creative force of the early Christian community.

[24]Ibid., 335. *Tertium non datur*—"There is no third choice."

[25]"The transfiguration had, in fact, been the revelation of the secret of the Messiahship to the three who constituted the inner circle of the disciples. And Jesus had not Himself revealed it to them; what had happened was, that in a state of rapture common to them all, in which they had seen the Master in a glorious transfiguration, they had seen Him talking with Moses and Elias and had heard a voice from heaven saying, 'This is my beloved Son, hear ye Him'" (ibid., 383–84).

[26]One detail in the gospel record does not fit Schweitzer's theory. In Mark, the Transfiguration actually occurs *after* Peter's confession! But Schweitzer simply insists, "To make the narrative coherent, the transfiguration, as being a revelation of the Messiahship, ought to precede the incident at Caesarea Philippi" (ibid., 381).

course. According to Schweitzer, Jesus himself tried to force events in order to hasten the Parousia, the coming of the Son of Man in his glory.

At his baptism, Jesus had a psychological, inner experience (Schweitzer is not prepared to allow for a visible miracle) that he interpreted as his being designated as the Messiah who would soon return on the clouds of heaven to establish the kingdom of God. From that time on, Jesus went about announcing that the kingdom was at hand. To proclaim that truth was Jesus' main task; his teaching was secondary. This explains how he could suddenly break off his teaching ministry altogether just as it seemed to be winning a following.

Like Johannes Weiss,[27] Schweitzer viewed Jesus' ethics as simply an *Interimsethik,* "the special ethic of the interval before the coming of the Kingdom." For this and other reasons, according to Schweitzer, Jesus' teaching is not very useful today. Schweitzer noted especially the predestinarian emphasis in Jesus' teaching, which is so "inconceivable" to modern men and women. "Many are invited, but few are chosen" (Matt. 22:14). Schweitzer acknowledged that this "predestinarian view goes along with the eschatology." He explained, "The kingdom cannot be 'earned'; what happens is that men are called to it, and show themselves to be called to it." Nevertheless, Schweitzer insisted, although a certain harmony between Jesus' eschatology and his predestinarianism can be recognized, these twin emphases remain at the heart of those elements in Jesus' teaching that make his outlook so alien, so strange and unhelpful to us.[28]

Although Jesus thought at first that it was his mission merely to announce the kingdom's coming, Matthew 10:23 points us to a turning point, according to Schweitzer.[29] As he sent the disciples out on their preaching mission, Jesus promised, "I tell you the truth, you will not finish going through the cities of Israel before the Son of Man comes." But that did not happen, and the nonfulfillment of Jesus' expectation became the crisis experience that determined the later part of Jesus' very brief ministry. (Schweitzer argued that Jesus' ministry lasted less than a year.) Jesus now

---

[27]See chap. 5, sec. 1, above.

[28]Schweitzer, *Quest of the Historical Jesus,* 352–53.

[29]Reimarus appealed to this same text. See p. 17, above.

abandoned the hope that the final tribulation would begin of itself. ... That meant—not that the Kingdom was not near at hand—but that God had appointed otherwise in regard to the time of trial. He had heard the Lord's Prayer in which Jesus and His followers prayed for the coming of the Kingdom—and at the same time, for deliverance from the *peirasmos*.[30] The time of trial was not come; therefore God in His mercy and omnipotence had eliminated it from the series of eschatological events, and appointed to Him whose commission had been to bring it about, instead to accomplish it in His own person. As He who was to rule over the members of the Kingdom in the future age, He was appointed to serve them in the present, to give His life for them, the many (Mark x.45 and xiv.24), and to make in His own blood the atonement which they would have had to render in the tribulation. The Kingdom could not come until the debt which weighed upon the world was discharged.[31]

He also explained: "The enigmatic *polloi* ["the many"] for whom Jesus dies are those predestined to the Kingdom, since His death must at last compel the Coming of the Kingdom. This thought Jesus found in the prophecies of Isaiah, which spoke of the suffering Servant of the Lord."[32]

Thus Schweitzer's view of Jesus' understanding was similar to Weiss's—not a ransom price of vicarious repentance, however, but more precisely of vicarious tribulation.

Because Jesus was consciously forcing the events, Schweitzer said, he could predict his suffering, death, and resurrection (Jesus' references to his resurrection being, according to Schweitzer, references to his Parousia). On the cross, however, came disillusionment. There Jesus despaired at last of ever bringing in the new heaven and the new earth.[33] That is how Schweitzer would have us understand Jesus' final cry—not as the shout of triumph, but as the recognition of defeat: "It is finished" (John 19:30). In the most dramatic and most often quoted passage in *The Quest of the Historical Jesus,* Schweitzer wrote:

---

[30]We usually translate the prayer in Matt. 6:13 as "lead us not into temptation," but Schweitzer is translating the Greek word that appears there *(peirasmos)* as "trial."

[31]Schweitzer, *Quest of the Historical Jesus,* 387.

[32]Ibid., 388.

[33]Ibid., 254.

There is silence all around. The Baptist appears, and cries: "Repent, for the Kingdom of Heaven is at hand." Soon after that comes Jesus, and in the knowledge that He is the coming Son of Man lays hold of the wheel of the world to set it moving on that last revolution which is to bring all ordinary history to a close. It refuses to turn, and He throws Himself upon it. Then it does turn; and crushes Him. Instead of bringing in the eschatological conditions, He has destroyed them. The wheel rolls onward, and the mangled body of the one immeasurably great Man, who was strong enough to think of Himself as the spiritual ruler of mankind and to bend history to His purpose, is hanging upon it still. That is His victory and His reign.[34]

"That is His victory and His reign"? The words sound pious, but what can they mean in the context of Schweitzer's view of the historical Jesus? Why should this megalomaniac, who could "think of Himself as the spiritual ruler of mankind," be considered "immeasurably great"? Schweitzer assured his readers that, "like every great tragedy,"[35] Jesus' tragic death had great results. What were they?

What Schweitzer offered as a positive assessment of the value of Jesus for us today was remarkably similar to the thinking of the Hegelian critics six decades earlier.[36] We may wish that Jesus had preached pure religious Ideas completely divorced from the eschatological concepts (Forms) of the religious world in which he lived, but this is to desire the impossibly ahistorical. What we must do is clothe Jesus' true religion of love in the thought-forms of our modern world-and-life view. The liberals had attempted to do this, naively and covertly, Schweitzer charged, in defiance of what the gospel text actually said. We must now do so openly and candidly, leaving behind once and for all the eschatological, supernatural faith of the historical Jesus, who must always remain "to our time a stranger and an enigma."[37] Jesus displayed no concern to spiritualize the Jewish

---

[34]Ibid., 368–69.

[35]Ibid., 254.

[36]See chap. 2, above.

[37]Schweitzer, *Quest of the Historical Jesus*, 397. The strong emphasis on the eschatology of the historical Jesus by such twentieth-century critics as Weiss, Schweitzer, and Bultmann results not in the affirmation of that eschatology, but rather in the complete repudiation and abandonment of it. As noted earlier, their exegetical conclusions that

hopes regarding God's kingdom, but it is Christianity's task constantly to spiritualize everything that comes its way.

Why this "spiritualized" (which for Schweitzer is another word for "desupernaturalized") religion of "pure love" and a vague "reverence for life" should continue to appeal to Jesus as its supreme model or hero was never made at all clear by Schweitzer.[38] The following excerpts from his concluding chapter represent Schweitzer's best effort to draw a meaningful connection between Jesus Christ and the religious life of those who continue to bear his name, but surely his "sermon" raises more questions than it answers:

> Those who are fond of talking about negative theology can find their account here. There is nothing more negative than the result of the critical study of the Life of Jesus. . . .
>
> . . . He will not be a Jesus Christ to whom the religion of the present can ascribe, according to its long-cherished custom, its own thoughts and ideas, as it did with the Jesus of its own making. . . .
>
> . . . The real immovable historical foundation [of Christianity] . . . is independent of any historical confirmation or justification.
>
> Jesus means something to our world because a mighty spiritual force streams forth from Him and flows through our time also. This fact can neither be shaken nor confirmed by any historical discovery. It is the solid foundation of Christianity. . . .
>
> . . . [W]e must be prepared to find that the historical knowledge of the personality and life of Jesus will not be a help, but perhaps even an offence to religion.
>
> But the truth is, it is not Jesus as historically known, but Jesus as spiritually arisen within men, who is significant for our time and can help it. . . .
>
> The abiding and eternal in Jesus is absolutely independent of historical knowledge and can only be understood by contact with His spirit which is still at work in the world.[39]

---

have at least the appearance of a certain advance beyond liberalism have led to no theological gain at all.

[38]We shall see later that this is also the central criticism that has been made with regard to the most influential New Testament critic of our century, Rudolf Bultmann, by both his theological friends and his foes.

[39]Schweitzer, 396–97, 399.

While many have praised Schweitzer's book as a key factor in bringing an end to the "old" quest of the historical Jesus, virtually no one has followed his interpretation of Jesus. No "Schweitzerian school" has arisen—and for obvious reasons. While Schweitzer offered a certain degree of exegetical advance over Ritschlian liberalism and attempted to deal more seriously with the gospel records, even affirming the historical accuracy of many details previously questioned, his overall interpretation is obviously and grossly one-sided. As presented in the Gospels, Jesus' concept of messiahship and the kingdom is not exclusively occupied with the future. (C. H. Dodd's later study of the parables, for example, made this abundantly clear. Unfortunately, Dodd allowed the pendulum of interpretation to swing all the way to the opposite extreme of totally "realized" eschatology and missed the presence of both "already" and "not yet" elements in Jesus' kingdom teaching.[40])

To a great extent, Schweitzer was out of step with the just-emerging twentieth-century approach to Gospels criticism, which I have regularly referred to as radicalism, and which has tended to place the greatest emphasis on the religious genius and creative force of the early Christian community rather than on Jesus himself.

Certainly Schweitzer's Jesus was not one that the common person could find appealing. Rather than being a "winning personality," Schweitzer's Jesus is a repellent figure, dominated in all his thoughts and actions by a prodigious error. But the fact is that, for the most part, men and women find themselves irresistibly attracted to Jesus in some way. Most people do not easily come to the point of utterly rejecting and repudiating Jesus, but most would find it necessary to do so if Schweitzer's portrait of him were accurate. Thus, Schweitzer's interpretation of the Gospels did not appeal to readers—although his view of religion and his personal example of sacrificial service to others certainly did.

---

[40]C. H. Dodd, *The Parables of the Kingdom* (London: James Nisbet, 1935).

PART THREE:
BULTMANN AND BEYOND

6

Martin Kähler (1835–1912): Forerunner?

Aт this point, our survey makes a significant departure from chronological order. We have already considered important studies published
by William Wrede in 1901, by Albert Schweitzer in 1906, and by
Wilhelm Bousset in 1913. Now, however, we return to 1892 (the same
year that Johannes Weiss published his treatise on Jesus' proclamation
of the kingdom[1]) to note a brief work that was largely ignored when it
first appeared,[2] but which has come to be viewed by many as ranking
alongside the writings of David Strauss and Rudolf Bultmann in the
very top echelon of groundbreaking works in the history of Gospels
criticism. Certainly it reopened in a distinctive way that most crucial
of all theological issues relating to the study of the Gospels, namely,
the question of the relationship between an assured faith and the
uncertainties of history—the question that has continued to occupy
Christian thought throughout the twentieth century.

There would seem to be several reasons why surveys of Gospels
criticism find it difficult to decide where to insert a consideration of

---

[1]See pp. 76–77, above.
[2]Norman Perrin, *Rediscovering the Teaching of Jesus* (New York: Harper & Row,
1967), 216.

89

Martin Kähler[3] (if they take him up at all): (1) Kähler's thought seems to have been, in the final analysis, quite original and independent of the various schools of theology in his day. (2) As noted above, Kähler seems to have made no impact on Gospels criticism at the time. Schweitzer does not even mention Kähler's treatise in his classic survey published fourteen years later. Geerhardus Vos makes no reference to Kähler in his 1926 study. (3) Kähler's thought is not easy to understand at all points and has given rise to quite different interpretations, and thus to different notions as to where it "fits" in the history of Gospels criticism.[4] (4) The most enthusiastic expressions of appreciation for Kähler's thought have come after his death,[5] from the exponents of twentieth-century "kerygma theology" (first in its Barthian form and later in its Bultmannian)—even though it seems clear that they have used his key terms with meanings quite different from his, and have reached radically negative conclusions with regard to the historicity of the picture of Jesus given in the Gospels, quite opposed to Kähler's own convictions.[6]

If we may make use of Kähler's famous distinction between the "historical" and the "historic," in the sense in which that distinction has become popular (although, as we shall see, that is significantly different from the sense in which Kähler himself intended that distinction),

---

[3]Martin Kähler was a systematic theologian at Halle. He had studied theology at Heidelberg, Tübingen, and Halle, and once referred to his New Testament studies at Tübingen under F. C. Baur as his "critical cold water bath."

[4]Harvey K. McArthur is of the opinion that "Kähler's language was not always clear, and this may reflect confusions in his own thought" (*The Quest Through the Centuries* [Philadelphia: Fortress, 1966], 118).

[5]Kähler's key treatise (first published in 1892) was not translated into English (from the 1896 edition) until 1964.

[6]Paul Althaus: "Bultmann has taken over Kähler's terminology, not without a sinister change of meaning" (*The So-called Kerygma and the Historical Jesus,* trans. David Cairns [Edinburgh: Oliver and Boyd, 1959], 21).

Norman Perrin is an example of one who misses that change of meaning in Bultmann's use of Kähler's terminology. Perrin presents Kähler as though he were a Bultmannian before Bultmann! In affirming that Kähler "restated" and Bultmann "maintained" the "reformation principle . . . [that] faith as such is necessarily independent of historical facts, even historical facts about Jesus" (*Rediscovering the Teaching of Jesus,* 221), Perrin is true to neither Kähler nor the Reformers.

we might say that the "historical" Martin Kähler (that is, Martin Kähler as he really thought and taught in his lifetime) must be understood in terms of his own historical context (with liberalism and the life-of-Jesus movement in the ascendancy), whereas the "historic" Kähler (that is, Martin Kähler as his terms and concepts have been adopted and become influential in the twentieth century) must be understood in terms of Barth, Bultmann, and their followers.[7]

The basic thesis of Kähler's rather brief treatise was highlighted in its title: *Der sogenannte historische Jesus und der geschichtliche, biblische Christus* [The so-called historical Jesus and the historic, biblical Christ]. Early in that essay it becomes clear that Kähler considers the "historical" Jesus—"so-called"—to be a figment of the scholar's imagination, "merely a modern example of human creativity."[8]

Why? For a correct understanding of Kähler, the correct answer to this question is absolutely crucial. Why did Kähler consider the search for the so-called historical Jesus to be a blind alley? What did Kähler mean when he spoke of the *historische* ("historical") Jesus? Was he referring by that term to the Jesus who "really lived"—and when he insisted that the search for such a Jesus was "a blind alley," was he saying that a Jesus who really lived never existed, or, if he did, that the facts concerning him (what he was, what he said, what he did) are theologically insignificant? No, not at all. Affirming the theological insignificance of the particulars of the Jesus of history would accord with the theology of Rudolf Bultmann, whose views we shall consider in our next chapter (and who appealed to Kähler at this point), but it would not be in harmony with the theology of Martin Kähler.

What Kähler called "the so-called historical Jesus" was the Jesus portrayed in the then popular, usually liberal, life-of-Jesus literature. It was "this whole 'Life of Jesus movement'" that Kähler declared

---

[7]Rudolf Bultmann and his leading disciples will be considered in the following chapters. Karl Barth will not be treated in this brief survey, in spite of his enormous influence on twentieth-century theology generally, because he contributed little to the subject of Gospels criticism.

[8]Martin Kähler, *The So-called Historical Jesus and the Historic Biblical Christ*, trans. Carl E. Braaten (Philadelphia: Fortress, 1964), 43.

to be "a blind alley,"[9] because it sought the "real" Jesus by using the accepted methods of modern historical and literary criticism.[10] As Kähler saw it, these methods were simply not adequate to the task.

Kähler insisted that the "historic" *(geschichtliche)* Christ—i.e., the Christ who has been so significant in history, the Christ worshiped by the Christian church, the biblical Christ, the preached Christ—is the *real* Christ, and the *historical* Christ, if by "historical" is meant the Jesus Christ who really lived.

But, to emphasize the point again, the "historical Jesus" referred to by Kähler in his title is not the actual earthly Jesus, but the Jesus who has been discovered by the reconstructive methods of historical-critical research.[11] As Leander Keck well expresses it, the so-called historical Jesus is "the historian's Jesus."[12] Kähler's treatise and its title are misused when they are appealed to in support of a twentieth-century distinction between "the Jesus of history" and "the Christ of faith."

---

[9]Ibid., 46.

[10]Review Ernst Troeltsch's summary of the three primary principles of the historical-critical method, cited in the Introduction on pages 7ff., above.

[11]"The 'historical Jesus' is not the earthly Jesus as such, but rather Jesus insofar as he can be made the object of historical-critical research. The term has primary reference to the problem of historical knowledge, and does not intend to deny or devalue the historicity of revelation" (Carl E. Braaten, "Introduction," in Kähler, *So-called Historical Jesus,* 20–21).

Pannenberg was quite incorrect in saying that Kähler taught "that the real content of faith is suprahistorical" in the sense in which that affirmation "still lives today especially in the form of Barth's interpretation." Interestingly enough, Kähler's use of *Historie* was actually the same, I believe, as that of Pannenberg himself. Pannenberg explained his own usage as follows: "When I distinguish between history as *Geschichte* and as *Historie,* I understand by *Historie,* as H. Diem puts it, 'not the history which happened as such' with its own peculiar structure of reality, 'but the *historein* of this history' in the sense of the 'becoming-acquainted-with and bringing-into-experience and reporting on that which is experienced'" (Wolfhart Pannenberg, *Basic Questions in Theology,* vol. 1, trans. George H. Kehm [Philadelphia: Fortress, 1970], 15, 21).

Kähler did speak often of the "suprahistorical" when referring to Christ. By that term, however, he was not referring to that which is *geschichtlich* in the later neo-orthodox sense (that which is somehow "above" or "beyond" ordinary history), but rather to that which is supernatural, but which by the wonder of the Incarnation entered history.

[12]Leander E. Keck, *A Future for the Historical Jesus* (Nashville: Abingdon, 1971), 48.

Kähler would have agreed fully with this statement by B. B. Warfield (cited in our introduction, above): "It is the desupernaturalized Jesus which is the mythical Jesus, who never had any existence, the postulation of the existence of whom explains nothing and leaves the whole historical development hanging in the air."[13]

If it is correct that Kähler's study made little immediate impact, Braaten may have overstated the case somewhat in saying, "In retrospect we can see that Albert Schweitzer's *The Quest of the Historical Jesus,* 1906, served as an impressive scientific obituary to a movement which fourteen years earlier had been mortally wounded by Kähler's prophetic pen."[14] But it is certainly true that Kähler's arguments against the many attempts in the late nineteenth century to write a life of Jesus[15] were devastating. Kähler insisted that neither the gospel sources nor the historian's naturalistic methods were adequate to produce a biography of the real Jesus.

Kähler readily acknowledged that we possess no historical sources for Jesus' life that measure up to the criteria of reliability and adequacy required by the science of modern historiography for the construction of a biography. (Kähler added that "a trustworthy picture of the Savior for believers is a very different thing, and of this more will be said later.") The earliest documents that have come down to us were all written by believers in Christ, and "they tell us only about the shortest and last period of his life." In Kähler's purposefully "provocative" phrase, "one could call the Gospels passion narratives with extended introductions."[16]

Certainly the material necessary for understanding the psychology of Jesus is not in our possession:

> Does the true humanity of Jesus not demand that we understand how he grew, his gradual development as a religious genius, the breakthrough of his moral independence, the dawning and illumination of his messianic consciousness? The sources, however, contain

---

[13]See p. 9, footnote 11.

[14]Carl E. Braaten and Roy A. Harrisville, eds., *The Historical Jesus and the Kerygmatic Christ* (New York: Abingdon, 1964), 79.

[15]Review especially p. 48, above.

[16]Kähler, *So-called Historical Jesus,* 48, 48–49, 80.

nothing of all that, absolutely nothing! . . . The New Testament presentations were not written for the purpose of describing how Jesus developed.[17]

And most tellingly of all, Kähler emphasized how impossible it is to discover the "real" Jesus by the principle of analogy if the real Jesus is the incarnate, sinless Son of God:

> Is this method justified in writing about Jesus? Will anyone who has had the impression of being encountered by that unique sinless person . . . still venture to use the principle of analogy here once he has thoroughly assessed the situation? . . . The distinction between Jesus Christ and ourselves is not one of degree, but of kind. . . . The inner development of a sinless person is as inconceivable to us as life on the Sandwich Islands is to a Laplander. . . . All this is a miracle which cannot be explained merely in terms of an innocent disposition. It is conceivable only because this infant entered upon his earthly existence with a prior endowment quite different from our own . . . because God's grace and truth became incarnate in him. In view of this fact we would all do well to refrain from depicting his inner life by the principle of analogy. . . . The question is whether the historian will humble himself before the unique sinless Person—the only proper attitude in the presence of the norm of all morality.[18]

And just as psychological analogy will not suffice to disclose the real Jesus, neither will the principle of historical analogy so dear to the history-of-religions school. Kähler asked his readers to compare Paul and Jesus:

> On the one hand we see the true Jew, so profoundly and indelibly influenced by the cultural forces of his people and epoch; on the other hand we see the Son of Man, whose person and work convey the impression of one who lived as it were, in the timeless age of the patriarch. Thus a return to the first century does not appear to be very promising.[19]

---

[17]Ibid., 50, 51.
[18]Ibid., 53–55.
[19]Ibid., 54.

By making clear the impossibility of discovering the incarnate Son of God by the canons of naturalistic literary and historical criticism, Kähler sought to deliver Christian believers from the tyranny of the expert, the papacy of the professors: "Should we expect [believers] to rely on the authority of learned men when the matter concerns the source from which they are to draw the truth for their lives?"[20] Drawing attention to what Troeltsch would later refer to as the critical principle of methodological doubt, and echoing the famous statements of Gotthold Lessing[21] and Søren Kierkegaard[22] before him, Kähler wrote, "I cannot find sure footing in probabilities or in a shifting mass of details the reliability of which is constantly changing."[23]

Christian believers need a sure anchor for their faith, a safe harbor, a *sturmfreies Gebiet* (a storm-free, invulnerable area). Where did Kähler find that unassailable foundation for his and every believer's faith? *In Christ alone!* With his Lutheran forefathers, and the apostle Paul before them, Kähler trumpeted the good news of justification by faith alone in Christ alone. And the Christ who is the object of saving faith is the *preached* Christ, who is the *biblical* Christ, who alone is the *real* Christ.

To this point it seems easy to understand why in Kähler's own day "in a very general way he was counted among the biblicists and pietists."[24] What may seem more difficult to understand is why in our century Kähler has been appreciated and quoted primarily by theologians clearly opposed to evangelical, biblical Christianity, such as Paul Tillich, who "as one of the few surviving students of Martin Kähler,"

---

[20]Ibid., 109.

[21]In 1778 Lessing had pictured the gap between the accidental truths of history and the necessary truths of reason as "the ugly ditch which I cannot get across, however often and however earnestly I have tried to make the leap" ("On the Proof of the Spirit and of Power," *Lessing's Theological Writings,* trans. Henry Chadwick [London: Adam and Charles Black, 1956], 55).

[22]"How can something of an historical nature be decisive for an eternal happiness?" *Kierkegaard's Concluding Unscientific Postscript,* trans. David F. Swenson and Walter Lowrie (Princeton: Princeton University Press, 1944), 86.

[23]Kähler, *So-called Historical Jesus,* 111.

[24]Braaten, "Introduction," in Kähler, *So-called Historical Jesus,* 2.

was asked to write the foreword to the English translation of *The So-called Historical Jesus and the Historic Biblical Christ.*[25]

One reason that such modernist theologians have a sympathetic interest in Martin Kähler is that he clearly and vigorously rejected what he called the "authoritarian" faith of a Christian orthodoxy committed to the verbal inspiration and therefore the inerrancy of the Bible. The latter part of Kähler's first essay (following the first section) and the entire second essay are primarily an extended discussion of the nature of the Bible's authority. Kähler introduced the subject by asking the following questions:

> Must we simply accept the statements of the apostles and the New Testament, taking these as the limits of theology, now and hence-forth? Is this the way we must always proceed, that we continue to subscribe an *authoritarian faith* in relation to the Bible in spite of the questions the critics have raised regarding the origin of the biblical writings and the reliability of their statements?[26]

Clearly, Kähler anticipated a negative answer to these questions.

Kähler's treatise has received considerable attention from Wolfhart Pannenberg, a leading twentieth-century theologian (for example, in *Basic Questions in Theology,* vol. 1), because he is seeking to answer the same question that Kähler addressed, namely, how can one be a biblical Christian without taking the biblical view of the Bible?

Putting the question that way—assuming the church's histori-cally orthodox view of the Bible to be the biblical view—might be considered prejudicial. However, it would be beyond the scope of this survey to establish the biblical basis of the orthodox doctrine of Scrip-ture. Furthermore, Pannenberg makes clear that the historical doctrine of Scripture was Martin Luther's doctrine:

> Luther was still unable to make the distinction which is unavoidable today between the witness of Scripture and an event attested by it. For

---

[25]It should be noted, however, that while Tillich expressed his "joy in the fact that a kind of Kähler revival is taking place," he also said: "I do not believe that Kähler's answer to the question of the historical Jesus is sufficient for our situation today" (in Kähler, *So-called Historical Jesus,* vii, viii).

[26]Kähler, *So-called Historical Jesus,* 72.

him, history, the witness of Scripture, and doctrine still coincided. . . . [Luther] straightway designates the literal interpretation of Scripture as historical.[27]

And, in Pannenberg's estimation, "the dissolution of the traditional doctrine of Scripture constitutes a crisis at the very foundation of modern Protestant theology."[28] It is not surprising, therefore, that Pannenberg and other modern theologians have been drawn to Kähler's earnest attempt to resolve that crisis.

Kähler declared as emphatically as Pannenberg that the concept of an infallibly authoritative Bible—even though that was the church's historic view—could no longer be maintained. He derided the notion "that only the inerrancy of Scripture concerning every incidental matter mentioned by the biblical writers could guarantee the trustworthiness of the one and only main point." He thanked Johann Tobias Beck for teaching him "to approach the Bible and to hold to it without detailed theories about its nature and origin." He spoke of the gospel tradition as "inherently fallible." Rather than viewing the Bible as one form in which the Word of God has come to us (the *written* Word of God), he made a sharp distinction between the Bible and the Word of God by speaking of the Bible as "the book within which we seek God's Word" and as the book which "contains God's revelation."[29]

Nevertheless, Kähler maintained that the Bible is both our *only* means and a fully *sufficient* means of coming to the "safe harbor" of faith in the living Christ, the Son of God, the Savior of sinners. He insisted that Christ

> is always—clearly or obscurely, but ultimately—the Christ of the Bible. The more converse a person has with the Bible itself, the more he finds that the drawing power of the Savior merges with the authority of the Bible. Because his Christ is the biblical Christ, and because his realization grows that he has the Bible to thank for his Christ, the Christian comes to believe that he has received not only this Christ but also his faith from the Bible.[30]

---

[27]Pannenberg, *Basic Questions in Theology,* 1:61.
[28]Ibid., 4.
[29]Kähler, *So-called Historical Jesus,* 91, 106, 112–14.
[30]Ibid., 76.

And yet, again and again, he backed away from the thought that I can trust in this Savior and in his love for me *because,* in the words of the children's hymn, "the Bible tells me so": "No one has an independent faith of the kind and quality attested by the New Testament if he cannot say to the New Testament writers what the Samaritans said to the woman, 'It is no longer because of your words that we believe' (John 4:42)."[31]

From such statements it might be inferred that Kähler was contending for something of an "authority circle," in which the "internal testimony of the Holy Spirit"[32] elicits the believer's faith in both the Bible as the "breathed-out" Word of God (2 Tim. 3:16) and in its Christ as the incarnate Word (John 1:14)—something akin to the statement in the Westminster Confession of Faith that it is by that "saving faith" which "is the work of the Spirit of Christ" in believers' hearts that "a Christian believeth to be true whatsoever is revealed in the Word, for the authority of God Himself speaking therein," but that "the principal acts of saving faith are accepting, receiving, and resting upon Christ alone for justification, sanctification, and eternal life" (14.2). After all, in the quotation above, Kähler declared that "the drawing power of the Savior merges with the authority of the Bible." On the previous page he had written that "the Christian's faith in Christ and his trust in this unique book are inseparably intermeshed in the high esteem in which he has come to hold the Bible."[33] And later he affirmed that "in reality . . . we are not able to separate Christ and the Bible," and thus "the maturing Christian finds that the distinction

---

[31]Ibid., 76–77.

[32]To use the Reformers' phrase, which Kähler also used. Kähler emphasized that this testimony of the Holy Spirit has reference primarily to "the testimony which the Spirit gives *in the church* concerning the written word of God. This testimony is frequently instrumental in engendering the testimony of the Spirit in the hearts of individual believers (the testimony which is usually exclusively stressed); in any case, it confirms, supplements, and supports that testimony." Kähler spoke of the Spirit's testimony "concerning the written word of God," and not simply concerning its Christ, and he went on to insist that "what called forth and constituted the Reformation and every new awakening in our churches has always been the revival of faith in, and of preaching from, the written word of God" (Kähler, *So-called Historical Jesus,* 138–39).

[33]Ibid., 75.

between 'through' the Bible and 'for the sake' of Christ . . . finally loses its significance."[34]

It is therefore clear that Kähler labored hard to establish as "high" a view of the Bible as possible, apart from a recognition of its absolute authority as the fully inspired Word of God written. Indeed, he spoke of a certain preference for the church's traditional view of the Bible as compared to the modern one: "The old doctrine of the inspiration of the Bible is much closer than the one currently popular both to the intention which is dominant in the Bible itself and to what the church has experienced as a result of its possession of this collection."[35] He also declared that "we have been hasty in following Lessing's counsel to read the Bible as we read other books."[36]

Nevertheless, Kähler repeatedly emphasized that ultimately our faith must rest in Christ *alone,* and for Kähler that meant that ultimately faith could receive nothing as true simply because it is taught in the Bible: "When it finally comes to making a distinction, it will be clear to the Christian that 'we do not believe in Christ for the sake of the Bible but in the Bible for the sake of Christ.'"[37] He again declared, "We want to make absolutely clear that ultimately we believe in Christ, not on account of any authority, but because he himself evokes such faith from us."[38]

According to Kähler, the Bible accomplishes its God-intended purpose if it presents us with a generally reliable picture of Christ—the historic Christ, who is also the Christ who was actually born into our world and our history, lived, died, and arose from the dead. And this the Gospels undoubtedly give us:

> The biblical picture of Christ, so lifelike and unique beyond imagination, is not a poetic idealization originating in the human mind. The reality of Christ himself has left its ineffaceable impress upon this picture. . . .

---

[34]Ibid., 86–87.

[35]Ibid., 125.

[36]Ibid., 123.

[37]Ibid., 75. In the footnote on page 75, Kähler attributes the quoted affirmation to an unpublished sermon by Heinrich Hoffmann of Halle.

[38]Ibid., 87.

. . . Nowhere in the Gospels do we detect a rigorous striving for accuracy of observation or for preservation of detail. . . .

Nevertheless, from these fragmentary traditions, these half-understood recollections, these portrayals colored by the writers' individual personalities, these heartfelt confessions, these sermons proclaiming him as Savior, there gazes upon us a vivid and coherent image of a Man, an image we never fail to recognize. Hence, we may conclude that in his unique and powerful personality and by his incomparable deeds and life (including his resurrection appearances) this Man has engraved his image on the mind and memory of his followers with such sharp and deeply etched features that it could be neither obliterated nor distorted. . . .

. . . [T]his diaphanous medium is not a nebulous legend but a tangible human life, portrayed in a rich and concrete though brief and concise manner. . . .

. . . Once the infallibility of our biblical records is no longer demanded, then their comparatively remarkable trustworthiness will again be appreciated, even the trustworthiness of the legends, so far as this is conceivable.[39]

Kähler insisted that

a person who holds this view stands just as solidly upon the authority of the Bible as does any advocate of verbal inspiration—except that he does not have to take upon himself the burden of proving the details of the tradition regarding the biblical books, a burden always acknowledged by the advocates of verbal inspiration.[40]

In his attack upon liberalism and the life-of-Jesus movement, in his refusal to join the search for a "real" Jesus "behind" the Jesus portrayed in the Gospels, Kähler surely had the best of intentions—and his key arguments still need to be voiced against such twentieth-century "neoliberals" as Wolfhart Pannenberg, who continues to insist that

the Christ-event must be distinguishable from the process of its—continually differing—proclamation. . . . Thus what is needed is precisely the historical quest, moving behind the kerygma [the New

---

[39]Ibid., 79, 89–90, 95, 141–42.
[40]Ibid., 140.

Testament preaching] in its various forms, into the public ministry, death, and resurrection of Jesus himself in order in that way to obtain in the Christ-event itself a standard by means of which to judge the various witnesses to it, even those actually within the New Testament.[41]

Kähler's good intentions, however, were ultimately thwarted by his refusal to take the fully biblical view of the Bible as well as the biblical view of Christ. As we shall go on now to consider the theology of those who claim to have been most influenced by Kähler, we shall have to conclude that he was quite naive in thinking that a recognition of some vague, undefined "comparatively remarkable trustworthiness" of the Gospels would prove an adequate foundation on which to build a faith in the historic, biblical Christ that would withstand the storms of biblical criticism. We have already indicated that the so-called kerygmatic theology of Rudolf Bultmann distorted Kähler's Christology, and it would be unfair to lay responsibility for such distortion at Kähler's door. Still, the radical turn given to Kähler's thought has exposed its basic weakness, namely its inadequate doctrine of Scripture. Paul Althaus notes that

> Luther, in his doctrine of holy scripture as the word of God, always presupposed, usually tacitly, the credibility of the book as a whole as the product of the Holy Spirit. . . .
> . . . For Luther, the principle *sola fide* is inconceivable without previously assumed certainty about Holy Scripture, its reliability, and consequently the historical reality of the history to which it bears witness.[42]

In order to have been the effective prophet of a Lutheran theological revival that he desired to be, Martin Kähler needed to affirm Luther's doctrine of Scripture as well as Luther's doctrine of Christ.

---

[41]Pannenberg, *Basic Questions in Theology,* 1:195–96.

[42]Althaus, *So-called Kerygma,* 50, 54. Althaus, unfortunately, but so typically in modern theology, rejects Luther's doctrine of the plenary inspiration of the Bible with a wave of the hand: "It is unnecessary to say that this theory is no longer tenable."

7

Rudolf Bultmann (1884–1976)

Rᴜᴅᴏʟꜰ Bᴜʟᴛᴍᴀɴɴ's great significance for Gospels criticism in the twentieth century is indicated in the very title chosen for Part Three of our survey: "Bultmann and Beyond." The thought of this longtime professor at Marburg has proved to be a watershed in New Testament studies in general and in the study of the Gospels in particular, and many who began their academic careers as his disciples have been in the forefront of efforts to move gospel studies farther along on the path he marked out.[1]

Bultmann was a pioneer in both New Testament critical methodology (as an advocate of the "science" of form criticism) and New

---

[1]The opinion expressed by Stephen Neill and Tom Wright in *The Interpretation of the New Testament,* 2d. ed. (Oxford: Oxford University Press, 1988), 237, that the Bultmannian school "is still the most powerful contemporary movement in New Testament interpretation," is certainly correct.

The authors go on to present this interesting summary of the background of Bultmann's thought, which we have previously surveyed: "We commented earlier on the fact that no ghosts are ever laid in Germany. In the writings of Bultmann we encounter the full procession of the ghosts. Here is Strauss telling us that the life of Christ cannot be written because the connecting thread between the individual events has been broken. Here is Baur, insisting on the radical difference between Jewish and

Testament theology (as he sought to bring Christian theology into harmony with modern existentialist philosophy, that of Martin Heidegger in particular).

1. Form Criticism

Norman Perrin has called form criticism "the single most important development in the history of" Gospels criticism, "for it provides what must be regarded as the only satisfactory understanding of the nature of the synoptic gospel material."[2] Form criticism (in German, *Formgeschichte*) claims to be a scientific method of getting behind any literary work to its origin, its solid historical foundation. It is alleged to be truly scientific because it avoids being subjective or arbitrary in its approach to the text.

Practitioners of the form-critical method of Gospels criticism may personally hold varying opinions regarding the significance of the person and work of Jesus of Nazareth, some being more conservative than others. All who would employ the method extensively, however, share the presupposition that is characteristic of what we have been calling "radical" criticism, that is, the presupposition that the early believing community was the great creative force in the origin of Christianity. Originally this method was a specific application of the principles of the broader history-of-religions school.[3]

Form criticism as a method of *biblical* criticism emerged in Germany at the close of World War I. The first to apply it to the Bible was Hermann Gunkel, who made use of it in his studies of the Old Testament, especially in the third edition of his commentary on Genesis, published in 1917. Rudolf Bultmann was one of three German professors who pioneered the use of this method in New Testament

---

Gentile Christianity. Here is Schweitzer . . . teaching us that Jesus of Nazareth supposed that the great act of God in him would mean the end of human history. Here is the radical scepticism of Wrede. Above all, here is the tradition of the religio-historical school as it was in Marburg in its flourishing days of seventy years ago" (pp. 237–38).

[2]Norman Perrin, *Rediscovering the Teaching of Jesus* (New York: Harper & Row, 1967), 218.

[3]See chap. 4, above.

study, particularly of the Synoptic Gospels. The other two were K. L. Schmidt and Martin Dibelius.[4]

This trio of New Testament scholars had important predecessors in Wrede, Bousset, and Wellhausen. Wrede had insisted that all the canonical gospels (including Mark) were theological rather than historical productions, which therefore told us more about the religious views of their authors than about those of Jesus.[5] Bousset had applied the *religionsgeschichtliche Methode* to the Gospels, and as a result had attributed much in them to Hellenistic Christianity.[6] Wellhausen had attempted an analysis of Q (a hypothetical document supposedly lying behind the synoptics), assuming that it was itself already an editorial product incorporating many levels of tradition. Their studies placed a great chasm between the Synoptic Gospels and the historical Jesus.

Bultmann (along with Dibelius and Schmidt) accepted their conclusions and extended them. Thus, the Gospels came to be viewed as sources for early church history, but hardly at all as sources for the teaching of Jesus.

The basic assumption of form criticism, with regard to any body of ancient literature, is that the earliest form of the tradition was oral, and that this oral tradition later shaped and produced the variety of literary forms found in the final written record. The goal of form criticism is to get "behind" the Gospels to the original oral form, in order to determine the origin of every bit of the tradition. Thus, form criticism wants to "dig deeper" than the earlier two-document theory

---

[4]Bultmann's influential work in this area was published in 1921, *Die Geschichte der synoptischen Tradition* (Göttingen: Vandenhoeck & Ruprecht, 1921). The second German edition (1931) was translated into English in 1963, and a revised edition was published in 1968: Rudolf Bultmann, *The History of the Synoptic Tradition,* trans. John Marsh (New York: Harper & Row, 1968). Karl Ludwig Schmidt and Martin Dibelius had both published their groundbreaking books two years earlier, in 1919. The revised second edition of Dibelius's *Die Formgeschichte des Evangeliums* (Tübingen: J. C. B. Mohr, 1933) was translated into English as *From Tradition to Gospel* (London: Ivor Nicholson and Watson, 1934). Schmidt's *Der Rahmen der Geschichte Jesu* [The framework of the story of Jesus] (Berlin: Trowitzsch & Sohn, 1919) has not been translated into English.

[5]Chap. 4, sec. 1, above.

[6]Chap. 4, sec. 2, above.

of gospel origins,[7] which, as its name indicated, limited its study to an examination of the two written documents thought to be the basis of our Synoptic Gospels: one extant document (Mark) and one presumably lost document (Q). For form criticism, the most significant work only begins at this point.

In form criticism, the Fourth Gospel is just about eliminated immediately as a historical record of Jesus' ministry, but the synoptics are viewed as something like a mosaic of pictures of Jesus that can yield historically accurate information if studied correctly. That study properly begins by shattering the framework of the mosaic, so to speak—the relationship in which the various elements of the Gospels stand to one another in our written accounts. Then the individual pieces of the mosaic should be examined individually, because (it is claimed) they were originally transmitted in the oral tradition in no particular relation to one another—perhaps something like the assorted facts that President Reagan was famous for carrying with him on index cards, which could be differently selected and arranged for different speeches.

Another metaphor often used is that of a necklace of beautifully matched pearls, which possesses a certain harmony as the individual pearls are strung together. This necklace may be likened to the Gospels as they now stand. Form criticism says that the critic must "break the string" in order to examine the "pearls" separately and come to a new estimate of their significance and of the true relation between them.

The form-critical method proceeds in three steps:

1. The various literary units are isolated from their context in the Gospels. Each unit is often called a pericope (a term derived from the Greek words meaning "to cut around") and defined as a passage (usually short) selected from a larger written work.

2. Using internal criticism, the isolated units are classified and categorized according to their literary form: parables, miracle stories, pronouncements, and so on. Certain laws of style are said to determine the classification. Here the history-of-religions method comes in, because the laws of style are gleaned from a study of the other literature of the period. The critic's evaluation of the religious climate of the

---

[7]See chap. 3, sec. 1, above.

times, and of the influences this climate had on the composition of the Gospels, determines how he will construct the various categories, the various literary "bins," shall we say, into which the different units are to be placed.

Note that as the units are classified, they are also reduced to their supposedly original form. More will be said on this in a moment.

3. Using external or historical criticism, the critic reconstructs the history of the early church and determines just where each of the literary units fits into that history. Those units that supposedly reflect situations that arose in the church after Jesus' death are eliminated from the history of Jesus as anachronistic.

(An obvious difficulty that might be noted here is that the critic himself has devised the categories—the forms—and has assigned historical value to them according to his idea of what the early history of the church actually was. Thus, a circular argument would seem to be inevitable.)

Three primary stages in the development of Christianity are generally recognized: (1) Jesus' own ministry, (2) the primitive, Palestinian church, (3) the Hellenistic church. As a result of his form-critical studies, Rudolf Bultmann assigned most of the material in our Gospels to the Hellenistic church, fewer elements to Palestinian Christianity, and very few to Jesus himself.

Let us now go back and look more carefully at each of the three steps in the form-critical method:

1. *The separation of the various units from their framework in the gospel record.* Form criticism insists that the framework of chronological, geographical, and topographical data given in the Gospels (*when* and *where* a particular event took place or particular teaching was given) was the work of the Evangelists (the gospel writers or editors). Therefore, it consists of artificial transitional links, not valid historical facts. The gospel tradition does not give us a continuous narrative or "biography" of Jesus, but only individual, isolated stories.[8]

---

[8]The passion narratives are commonly viewed by form critics as an exception at this point, because there seem to have been primitive connecting links in the telling of this story from the earliest times.

The element of truth here is that the Gospels are certainly not biographies in the modern sense.[9] They are gospels—that is, preaching of good news. They do not attempt to provide a comprehensive, or even an orderly, "life of Jesus." Think of the rather vague links provided by Mark, often consisting simply of the introductory Greek adverb *euthys* ("at once," or more indefinitely "so then"). The evangelists often arranged their material for didactic purposes, rather than chronological ones. Indeed, chronological data are rather rare and usually general. Evidently the gospel writers were not as interested in time and place as we might have expected. Often it seems that elements are not linked chronologically or geographically, but rather have been grouped on the basis of some other criterion—topically, perhaps. An example might be Matthew 9:35–10:42, where Matthew may have brought together elements of Jesus' teaching regarding the mission of his disciples—teaching given originally on different occasions in different contexts.[10] Obviously, this is an important point to remember in any attempt to produce a "harmony" of the Gospels.[11] Those liberals who professed to be able to trace the *development* in Jesus' life (H. J. Holtzmann being, perhaps, the leading example) were misreading the Gospels.

---

[9]Martin Kähler emphasized this point; see chap. 6, above. But even here Stephen Neill reminds us that "everything depends on definition. . . . [I]f it is the aim of biography to give succinctly a living and vivid impression of someone who really lived, it is hard to see into what other category the Gospels are to be placed" (Neill and Wright, *Interpretation of the New Testament,* 278).

[10]With the aid of a "synopsis" (such as *Synopsis of the Four Gospels,* ed. Kurt Aland, 8th ed. [Stuttgart: German Bible Society, 1987]), compare the contexts in which the parallels to this passage in Matthew appear in the other gospels.

[11]This one factor does not solve all the problems of harmonizing the Gospels, of course. Other important characteristics of the Gospels must be kept in mind also. The evidence in the Gospels themselves indicates that verbal inspiration by the Holy Spirit did not necessarily result in stenographic accuracy in the accounts at every point. And since Jesus' teaching ministry spanned many months, he probably taught the same thing, or used the same parable, more than once. Furthermore, certain incidental data may be explained by the *theological* point the Evangelist may have been making. With regard to Matt. 5:1, for example, Matthew may have been drawing attention to the fact that this new lawgiver is the One greater than Moses by accenting the location of this significant sermon on the mountain, rather than, perhaps, on "a level place" on the side of the mountain (Luke 6:17).

When treating the so-called sayings material, the form critic insists that the historical "scene" in each case is set forth merely as an opportunity to present Jesus' teaching. At Mark 2:23–28, for example, it is alleged that the confrontation with the Pharisees was simply invented in order to present the apothegm: "The Sabbath was made for man, not man for the Sabbath. So the Son of Man is Lord even of the Sabbath" (vv. 27–28).

It is indeed important to recognize that the setting in the Gospels often *is* apparently incidental, and that the important thing is Jesus' teaching. A good example would seem to be Mark 12:28ff., where the focus is on Jesus' affirmation of the two greatest commandments. In Mark 3:31–35, the reader might be left wondering, "What happened later between Jesus and his mother?" But Mark does not satisfy our curiosity on that point. That was not his *purpose* in recording that scene. Thus, it would be wrong for a preacher to build his sermon on details in the scene, or to speculate about details not recorded for us. Jesus' statement is the important thing to Mark (and to the Spirit who inspired him), and it is the preacher's task to apply Jesus' teaching to his hearers and their lives today.[12]

Note well, however, that if the Evangelists were not concerned to provide in meticulous detail the kind of connecting data so important to biographers, or if the historical setting was not the focus of their interest at particular points, this by no means implies that they were indifferent to historical fact. Too often this non sequitur is assumed by the form critic. The reality is quite to the contrary. Since the "good news" presented in the Gospels is the announcement of what Jesus Christ, God's incarnate Son, has *done,* there is necessarily in the Gospels an emphasis on, and a real concern for, historical fact.

Both C. H. Dodd and Rudolf Otto have insisted that the very earliest Christian missionaries did not carry with them mere "pieces" of the gospel story in unconnected fragments (on interchangeable index cards, as it were), but rather preached from the first a gospel

---

[12]An excellent guide here is Jay E. Adams, *Preaching with Purpose* (Phillipsburg, N.J.: Presbyterian and Reformed, 1982).

history, such as is presented in Peter's sermon recorded in Acts 10:34–43.[13] They announced what had *happened:*

> Such a preaching was necessarily and actually a complete unity. Its unity, however, was not expressed in the form of isolated sections of detached maxims, or in that of a detached miracle story, but the unity of a simple story of what this man had been, intended, effected, and done soteriologically.[14]

The apostolic message did involve an element of connection between the events announced, and once it is recognized that that historical framework was rather general, rather than detailed and closely formulated, it can be seen that the Gospels do not present divergent, contradictory frameworks.

2. *The classification of the gospel units by literary form on the basis of internal criticism.* As mentioned above, at this stage of form criticism the units are not only classified according to literary category, but also changed (reduced) to their supposedly original form. The reader of a modern commentary on the Gospels frequently finds the writer saying, "But what Jesus was originally reported to have said was . . ."—and the reader's reaction may be, "Wow, how does the commentator know that?! Is he omniscient?!"

Briefly, this is how conclusions regarding the allegedly original form of a pericope are reached. It is assumed that certain accretions (additions) came into the stories in the telling of them, and that the Evangelists modified the traditions according to their own interests. To identify the accretions, the critic simply applies certain stylistic laws derived from a study of other literature of the time (rabbinic, Hellenistic) and the evidence from other oral traditions. The two most important of such stylistic laws are:

a. Each literary form has a certain stereotyped character, whether it is a parable, an apothegm (a short, pithy saying of an instructive character), an admonition, or whatever. Each unit is complete in itself,

---

[13]C. H. Dodd, *The Apostolic Preaching* (New York: Harper, 1935), 27–29.

[14]Rudolf Otto, *The Kingdom of God and the Son of Man,* trans. Floyd V. Filson and Bertram Lee Woolf, rev. ed. (reprint, Boston: Starr King, 1957), 83–84.

rounded off stylistically, and self-explanatory. Therefore, anything that would suggest a connection with the larger context must be an accretion. (Here is the opposite of the hermeneutical principle that the more you know about the context, the better your interpretation of a particular text will be.)

b. The presence of specific details, such as the names of individuals, is a sign of secondary development. Originally, the stories or sayings had a more indefinite character. For example, Mark 2:19, according to Bultmann, is a brief parable, unobjectionable from a stylistic point of view: "How can the guests of the bridegroom fast while he is with them?" But verse 20 represents a desertion of the parabolic form and the insertion of an allegorical application to Jesus' ministry: "But the time will come when the bridegroom will be taken from them, and on that day they will fast." Thus, verse 20 is a later addition to the parable in its original, pure form.[15]

We must question, however, whether such rigid stylistic presuppositions are valid. Where the matter, the content, outweighed the form, could not Jesus have altered the form?

3. *This third step involves external or historical criticism.* With the completion of the second step, we are left with isolated bits of tradition. The original historical framework, the space-and-time context needed to help us understand the meaning of the individual units, has been cast aside—the string holding the pearls together has been cut—the frame holding together the pieces of the mosaic has been broken. Therefore, a new historical framework has to be constructed—a purely hypothetical one!

Bultmann spoke of three primary needs in the early church: (1) the need to present effective apologetic argument against both Jews and pagans, (2) the need to foster the ongoing missionary expansion of the church, and (3) the need to maintain church discipline. Other form critics have added to that list. Clearly there was a catechetical need in the early church, the need to instruct converts in the meaning of their new-found faith. There was the liturgical need of a new religious community that was no longer worshiping in the Jewish synagogue.

---

[15]Bultmann, *History of the Synoptic Tradition,* 199.

Young churches needed guidance on a host of issues relating to ethics and lifestyle. Should Christ's followers pay taxes to the state? What is the proper Christian position regarding divorce, military service, and Sabbath observance?

It is a basic premise of form criticism that if certain pericopes in the Gospels can be seen to have met certain of these needs in the early church, they must have been originally devised in order to fulfill those needs. With the rise of form criticism, the German phrase *Sitz im Leben* became most significant in Gospels criticism, referring to that "life situation" in the early church which gave rise to the particular story or saying in view.

For example, Bultmann concluded confidently that the account of Peter's confession at Caesarea Philippi was a legend originally formulated as a resurrection story in the Palestinian church, "where Peter was looked up to as the founder and leader of the Church," but that it later took the form we find in our gospels because of the need for strict discipline in the church (see the reference in Matt. 16:19 to "binding" and "loosing") at the time

> when an institutional authority of Church leaders had taken the place of the personal authority of Peter, which by conjecture could be the period after Agrippa's persecution, in which James, and very likely John too, the sons of Zebedee, were victims, and in which Peter was driven from Jerusalem.[16]

Why, however, does the fact that a need for discipline arose in the church necessarily imply that these words of Jesus were created by the church and "put into Jesus' mouth"? Can we not easily imagine the early church making an application of a statement actually made by her Lord—its usefulness thus explaining the preservation of such a story, perhaps, but by no means denying its historicity?

There is simply no objective basis for assuming that such a story, and such a saying, were born out of nothing to meet the church's situation. William F. Albright well spoke of the "vicious circles" evident in the work of the leading form critics.[17] We see the circular

---

[16]Ibid., 259, 141.

[17]William Foxwell Albright, *From the Stone Age to Christianity*, 2d ed. (Garden City, N.Y.: Doubleday, 1957), 382. On the next page, Albright adds this judgment:

reasoning at work, for example, in Bultmann's insistence that the antitheses of Matthew 5 ("But *I* say unto you . . . ") are historical, but that such a statement as verse 17 ("Do not think that I have come to abolish the Law or the Prophets; I have not come to abolish them but to fulfill them") represents a legalistic view in the early church and is an attempt to reconcile that view with Jesus' antinomian statements. That there was such a view in the early church is established on the basis of this text. That this text is not a statement of the historical Jesus is established on the basis of there being such a view in the early church![18]

Form critics speak of certain "criteria of authenticity," three of which have been much discussed: the criterion of dissimilarity, the criterion of coherence, and the criterion of multiple attestation.[19] These criteria identify features in the gospel text that indicate that a particular

---

"From the standpoint of the objective historian data cannot be disproved by criticism of the accidental literary framework in which they occur, unless there are solid independent reasons for rejecting the historicity of an appreciable number of other data found in the same framework."

[18]Bultmann, *History of the Synoptic Tradition,* 138, 146–49, 163.

[19]Norman Perrin in *Rediscovering the Teaching of Jesus,* 39–49, has presented perhaps the most influential description of these criteria from the perspective of a convinced Bultmannian. R. T. France, in "The Authenticity of the Sayings of Jesus," in *History, Criticism & Faith,* ed. Colin Brown (Downers Grove, Ill.: InterVarsity Press, 1977), 101–43; Robert H. Stein, in "The 'Criteria' for Authenticity," in *Gospel Perspectives,* vol. 1, ed. R. T. France and David Wenham (Sheffield: JSOT, 1980), 225–63; and Donald A. Hagner, in *New Testament Criticism and Interpretation* (Grand Rapids: Zondervan, 1991), ed. David Alan Black and David S. Dockery, 78–83, provide both description of the criteria and excellent critique from a conservative, evangelical perspective. The reader may wish to consult other helpful criticisms of form criticism that have appeared over the years, among them Morna Hooker, "On Using the Wrong Tool," *Theology* 75 (1972): 575–81; E. L. Mascall, *Theology and the Gospel of Christ* (London: SPCK, 1977); Eberhard Güttgemanns, *Candid Questions Concerning Gospel Form-Criticism,* trans. William G. Doty (Pittsburgh: Pickwick, 1979); and especially *The Gospel and the Gospels,* ed. Peter Stuhlmacher (Grand Rapids: Eerdmans, 1991), particularly the chapters by Peter Stuhlmacher, E. Earle Ellis, and Birger Gerhardsson. As Robert A. Guelich notes, however, in the "Introduction" to the last volume, in spite of the compelling criticisms that have been offered, in the work of the Jesus Seminar begun in 1985 under the direction of Robert Funk (which we described on pp. 1–3, above), "the fundamental assumptions of form criticism about the Gospel tradition and its development still obtain unquestioned" (p. xiv).

saying or a particular event goes back to the teaching and the career of Jesus of Nazareth himself.

Actually, the second and third of these criteria are extensions of the first. France calls that first criterion "the essential criterion, around which all others revolve."[20] And Perrin acknowledges that that first criterion, which he has labelled "the criterion of dissimilarity," is, for the consistent form critic, "the fundamental criterion for authenticity upon which all reconstructions of the teaching of Jesus must be built." Perrin briefly formulates that criterion as follows: "The earliest form of a saying we can reach may be regarded as authentic [that is, it was actually spoken by Jesus himself], if it can be shown to be dissimilar to characteristic emphases both of ancient Judaism and of the early Church."[21]

Form critics object when conservatives state that criterion in a way that makes it sound as though the form critics are saying that only statements that are dissimilar to anything in the thoughts and concerns of either the early church or of Judaism could possibly have been made by Jesus himself. The criterion of dissimilarity does not say that; it merely says that it is only with regard to such "dissimilar" statements that the critic can have a high degree of confidence with respect to their authenticity.

Nevertheless, the fact is that for such a radically skeptical form critic as Norman Perrin, the failure of a particular saying to measure up to the dissimilarity criterion results in the outright denial of its authenticity. As France notes, the fact is that "the presumption is that sayings which do not pass this test are not authentic. . . . In other words, *the criterion is used not only as a principle of validation but also as a principle of exclusion.*"[22] Perrin bears this out when he insists that *"the nature of the synoptic tradition is such that the burden of proof will be upon the claim to authenticity.* This means in effect that we must look for indications that the saying does not come from the Church, but from the historical Jesus."[23]

---

[20]France, "Authenticity of the Sayings," 108.

[21]Perrin, *Rediscovering the Teaching of Jesus* , 39.

[22]France, "Authenticity of the Sayings," 111 (France's italics).

[23]Perrin, *Rediscovering the Teaching of Jesus,* 39 (Perrin's italics).

Bultmann assumed the correctness of Bousset's reconstruction of early church history, emphasizing the basic threefold division noted above: Jesus' own ministry, the primitive Palestinian church, and the Hellenistic church. And on the basis of his form-critical method, emphasizing the *Sitz im Leben* of the church and the dissimilarity criterion, Bultmann concluded that all New Testament references to redemption and salvation, and to Jesus as divine Savior, arose in the Hellenistic church and could never have developed on Palestinian soil.

This criterion of dissimilarity, which guides contemporary form criticism, resembles Adolf von Harnack's famous principle for separating the "kernel" in Jesus' teaching from the "husk." In suggesting that only those ideas which were original with Jesus formed the "kernel" of his teaching, while all that he shared with his contemporaries could be considered dispensable "husk," Harnack, the liberal, was not suggesting (as form criticism does) that Jesus did not actually teach the "husk" concepts, but only that they possess no enduring relevance for our faith today.[24] And yet the liberal criterion for ethical and religious relevance is strikingly similar to the form-critical criterion for authenticity.

Surely the criterion of dissimilarity—which says in effect that we can confidently attribute a statement to Jesus *only if there is no other possible explanation for its origin!*—represents a radical methodological skepticism that cannot be reasonably defended. It is not a caricature to say that that criterion isolates and permits us to accept as authentic just those elements in Jesus' teaching which never seemed important to God's people before Jesus' birth or after his resurrection, and which therefore had absolutely no influence on the thinking of the Christian church! In divorcing the historical Jesus from everything that he held in common with Judaism, the criterion of dissimilarity eliminates Jesus' share in his heritage as a son of the covenant and eliminates his role as the hope of Israel, the fulfillment of the promises of God. And in divorcing Jesus from everything that he held in common with the early church, it eliminates precisely those elements in Jesus' life and teaching which had the greatest creative and formative effect in bringing into being the infant Christian community, the new Israel of God.

The believer may therefore find it difficult to conceive of any-

---

[24]See pp. 54–55, above.

thing positive about form criticism's contribution to gospel studies. Actually, however, there are certain emphases here that the Bible-believing Christian can appreciate and that need to be kept in mind. Certainly it is important to remember that there was a church before there were the four gospels. Evangelical Christians should be concerned not to isolate the Gospels from the faith of the early church. The Gospels are in no way "neutral" documents, seeking to present so-called objective history. The Evangelists were believers giving expression to their personal faith in Christ and seeking to win converts to that faith by the Spirit's working with the Word. They were also "churchmen," sensitive to the situation in the church in their day. Every reader of Paul's letters soon becomes aware of the "occasional" nature of his writings. The Gospels are not so obviously so, perhaps, but they too are in a sense occasional writings. Recall the prologue to Luke's Gospel (1:1–4). John the Baptist's prominence in John's Gospel may be due to the fact that misunderstandings about his relation to Jesus had arisen in the church. At many points we may be helped in our understanding of, and our preaching of, a certain passage in the Gospels by considering what purpose that passage may have been intended to serve in the church for which that gospel was written—because we can well expect that passage to serve the same purpose in the church today.

As George Ladd has observed, we can also note that "form criticism has made a substantial contribution to an evangelical understanding of the Gospels in a negative way."[25] By that Ladd means that the form-critical method has failed to discover a "purely historical" Jesus anywhere in our gospel accounts—that is, a Jesus who would fit the terms of the naturalistic, rationalistic definition of the truly historical, namely, the nonsupernatural. As we commented earlier, this can make a commentary written by a form critic such as Bultmann more helpful in bringing out the theological force of a particular text than the commentaries written by the earlier liberals.

For Bultmann himself, however, the result of his form-critical methodology was totally negative. Wolfhart Pannenberg has described such form criticism as

---

[25]George Eldon Ladd, *The New Testament and Criticism* (Grand Rapids: Eerdmans, 1967), 158.

a curious process: precisely by making the biblical witnesses to Christ itself [*sic*] the object of historical investigation, taking the Gospel texts as expressions of the primitive Christ-kerygma, the event to which they bore witness remained in the dark from a historical perspective. In every stratum of the text one always found again yet another testimony of the Christian community, and never made contact with Jesus himself and his fate, hardly even with his own words.[26]

Bultmann expressed his negative conclusion quite clearly: "I do indeed think that we can now know almost nothing concerning the life and personality of Jesus."[27] As Bultmann saw it, there is very little in the Gospels that is not either secondary accretion in the tradition or editorial addition by the Evangelist. The accounts of Jesus' birth, his temptation in the desert, his transfiguration, his miracles, his triumphal entry into Jerusalem, most of the story of his passion, his resurrection, his ascension—all are pure myth. Indeed, although Bultmann rejected out of hand Bruno Bauer's denial of the historicity of Jesus,[28] so little was Bultmann concerned about "Christ after the flesh" (2 Cor. 5:16 KJV)[29] that he could say that he would not mind if some preferred "to put the name of 'Jesus' always in quotation marks and let it stand as an abbreviation for the historical phenomenon with which we are concerned."[30]

---

[26]Wolfhart Pannenberg, *Basic Questions in Theology,* vol. 1, trans. George H. Kehm (Philadelphia: Fortress, 1970), 86.

[27]Rudolf Bultmann, *Jesus and the Word,* new ed., trans. Louise Pettibone Smith and Erminie Huntress Lantero (New York: Charles Scribner's Sons, 1934), 8.

[28]For Bauer's position, see chap. 2, sec. 2, above. Bultmann wrote: "Of course the doubt as to whether Jesus really existed is unfounded and not worth refutation. No sane person can doubt that Jesus stands as founder behind the historical movement whose first distinct stage is represented by the oldest Palestinian community. But how far that community preserved an objectively true picture of him and his message is another question. . . . [F]or our purpose it has no particular significance" *(Jesus and the Word,* 13–14).

[29]As many commentators on Bultmann have observed, however, "the passage from II Corinthians 5:16 ('We know Christ no more after the flesh') is here misused. The words *kata sarka* ['after the flesh'] do not go with the object 'Christ,' but with the verb 'know'" (Paul Althaus, *The So-called Kerygma and the Historical Jesus,* trans. David Cairns [Edinburgh: Oliver and Boyd, 1959], 35).

[30]Bultmann, *Jesus and the Word,* 14.

The historical Jesus' sole significance was that somehow he was responsible for the emergence of the Christian message. It is that message alone that is religiously significant, according to Bultmann.

2. Bultmann's Existentialist Theology

At this point, it might seem impossible that any positive Christian theology could be formulated by taking such an utterly skeptical attitude toward the historical veracity of the foundational documents of the church. Bultmann, however, had a positive theology, a gospel, to proclaim. He found the key to that theology in the teaching of the German existentialist philosopher Martin Heidegger (1889–1976), commonly classified as an atheist. According to Bultmann, Heideggerian existentialism and the New Testament both present the same understanding of man's plight. The only difference is that the New Testament also presents the solution, namely, *justification by faith alone.* (When considering Bultmann's theology, remember that his announced goal was to be a consistent Lutheran.)

Heidegger's great concern was with the ultimate question, the question of the essence of Being *(Sein).*[31] Man was viewed as that particular form of Being that can be designated *Dasein,* literally "being there." Heidegger accented the "thrownness" of *Dasein.* He is "just there," projected into nothing. But man recognizes that in his being he is on the road to not-being. Man is both *Dasein* and *Sein-zum-Tode,* "being-towards-death." Because the moment of his death is not known ahead of time, man is continually confronted with Nothingness. In man as the questioner of ultimate Being, Being and Nothingness intersect. Man becomes aware of this in the mood of *Angst* (anxiety), a nameless, objectless dread. Every *Dasein* spontaneously faces the question, "Why is there Something instead of Nothing? Why is there I instead of Nothing?"

---

[31]Heidegger's principal work, *Sein und Zeit,* first appeared in 1927. In 1962 the English translators called it "the most celebrated philosophical work which Germany has produced in this century" (Martin Heidegger, *Being and Time,* trans. John Macquarrie and Edward Robinson [New York: Harper & Row, 1962], 13).

But man seeks to escape the recognition of his true nature, the radical contingency of himself—that he can as easily not-be as be!— by living an inauthentic existence.[32] Inauthentic existence is the life of absorption in the everyday, being occupied with externals. It is flight from responsibility and from the horror of what Jean Paul Sartre called man's "terrible freedom." Inauthentic existence is living not as *Dasein* but as *Das Man,* the Anonymous One, mass man, whose sole activity is *Sorge* (care, concern) for the people and the things of the world.

How can one pass from such inauthentic existence into authentic existence—which means to be absolutely open to the future, to give up all securities, all "crutches," all safe harbors? Existentialism, although it had correctly analyzed the human condition, had no answer to that question, Bultmann thought. The question in theological terms was, "What must I do to be saved?" Only the kerygma (the preached Christian message) gives us the answer to that question.

And the answer, Bultmann said, is the Cross—which we find at the same time to be the Resurrection! To respond in faith to the preached Word is to be open to the future, to freely accept death and thus to die to every false support, to embrace uncertainty as integral to being, to recognize that living is deciding, that every moment is the moment of eschatological decision, and to be willing to decide for God and his will—which means to live all out for the Other, not merely to continually weigh the evidence and see what's in it for me.

It is the kerygma that calls for and makes possible this existential response, and that preaching of the Cross is the power of God unto salvation for everyone who believes, *whatever* the actual history of Jesus of Nazareth may have been.

Now, Bultmann's existentialist gospel may seem quite different from the message of the New Testament. But that is where Bultmann's program of demythologizing comes in. He insisted that the New Testament is indeed presenting his existential message, but that it does so in mythological terms in keeping with its prescientific world-and-life view—a view that is now totally unacceptable to modern men and women.

---

[32]It seems to be merely a matter of personal choice whether Heidegger's term *uneigentlich* is translated "inauthentic" or "unauthentic."

In Bultmann's relatively brief 1941 essay entitled "New Testament and Mythology," his "original manifesto" and still in many ways the most significant of his writings, Bultmann first presented "The Problem": "The cosmology of the New Testament is essentially mythical in character. The world is viewed as a three-storied structure, with the earth in the centre, the heaven above, and the underworld beneath."[33]

Bultmann then goes on to summarize the theology of the New Testament that is set in that mythical cosmological framework:

> This aeon is held in bondage by Satan, sin, and death (for "powers" is precisely what they are), and hastens towards its end. That end will come very soon, and will take the form of a cosmic catastrophe. . . . [T]he Judge will come from heaven, the dead will rise, the last judgement will take place, and men will enter into eternal salvation or damnation. . . . [T]he last time has now come. "In the fulness of time" God sent forth his Son, a pre-existent divine Being, who appears on earth as a man. He dies the death of a sinner on the cross and makes atonement for the sins of men. His resurrection marks the beginning of the cosmic catastrophe. Death, the consequence of Adam's sin, is abolished, and the daemonic forces are deprived of their power. The risen Christ is exalted to the right hand of God in heaven and made "Lord" and "King." He will come again on the clouds of heaven to complete the work of redemption, and the resurrection and judgment of men will follow.[34]

This may seem to be a fair summary of the teaching of the New Testament, but, Bultmann insisted, it is simply impossible for any modern person to believe such a message: *"Man's knowledge and mastery of the world* have advanced to such an extent through science and technology that it is no longer possible for anyone seriously to hold the New Testament view of the world—in fact, there is no one who

---

[33]Rudolf Bultmann et al., *Kerygma and Myth,* ed. Hans Werner Bartsch, rev. trans. Reginald H. Fuller (New York: Harper & Brothers, 1961), 1. All quotations from this essay are from this edition. The essay is also available in Rudolf Bultmann, *New Testament and Mythology and Other Basic Writings,* ed. and trans. Schubert M. Ogden (Philadelphia: Fortress, 1984), 1–43.

[34]Bultmann, *Kerygma and Myth,* 1–2.

does."[35] The New Testament eschatology is just as incredible as the New Testament cosmology, according to Bultmann: *"The mythical eschatology* is untenable for the simple reason that the parousia of Christ never took place as the New Testament expected. History did not come to an end, and, as every schoolboy knows, it will continue to run its course."[36]

What then is to be done? Should Christians attempt to delete the mythological elements in the New Testament as "husk," so that the "kernel" of truth might remain (as Harnack had suggested)? Well, not exactly, because, as Bultmann saw it (and here is where his radicalism differed sharply from the earlier liberalism), the whole New Testament message is "husk" in the sense that it is mythological *in toto,* whereas at the same time that message is at a deeper level "kernel." It is the truth that sets men free! To delete the mythological elements from the New Testament would be to delete the core of its teaching, the kerygma.

What must be done, according to Bultmann, is not to delete but to transform that kerygma into the conceptual framework with which modern people operate. That demythologization is to be accomplished by existentializing the New Testament message. Thus, the demythologization of the New Testament may be described as decontextualization and recontextualization. We must understand New Testament mythology, Bultmann insisted, not cosmologically but anthropologically, or, more specifically, existentially.

In the second half of his much-debated essay, Bultmann presented that "existentialist unmythological interpretation of the Christian understanding." After summarizing that new interpretation, he suggested that "the crux of the matter . . . comes to this: can we have a Christian understanding of Being without Christ?" Bultmann concluded that the answer to that question is "yes," and that the "startling" thing is that existentialism (and "above all" Heidegger) "is saying the same thing as the New Testament and saying it quite independently."[37] The reader can almost hear Bultmann at this point shouting out, "Eureka!"

---

[35]Ibid., 4 (Bultmann's italics).
[36]Ibid., 5 (Bultmann's italics).
[37]Ibid., 22–25.

Should we therefore simply abandon the Christian faith as a confused and confusing version of the clearer vision of Heideggerian existentialism? No, not at all, said Bultmann, because of the vital difference between the two that was mentioned earlier. While existentialism has correctly understood man's fate, it has not grasped the solution to his problem. Existentialist philosophers are

> convinced that all we need is to be told about the "nature" of man in order to realize it. . . . [T]his is the point where they part company with the New Testament. For the latter affirms the total incapacity of man to release himself from his fallen state. That deliverance can come only by an act of God.

Thus, "the only reasonable attitude for man to adopt apart from Christ is one of despair, to despair of the possibility of his ever achieving authentic Being." Bultmann continued:

> Here then is the crucial distinction between the New Testament and existentialism, between the Christian faith and the natural understanding of Being. The New Testament speaks and faith knows of an act of God through which man becomes capable of self-commitment, capable of faith and love, of his authentic life.[38]

How did Bultmann understand that "act of God" which the Christian kerygma announces? Here is where Bultmann was least clear, and here is where his critics have been most critical of his theological proposal. As we shall see in our next chapter, Bultmannian disciples to the theological left of their teacher have insisted that any reference to an "act of God" in human history reflects a nondemythologized surd in Bultmann's theology. Critics on the theological right insist that Bultmann never made clear how the act of God in Christ was an act of God *in history.*

Bultmann spoke of this redemptive act of God as "the event of Christ." And he described it as "a unique combination of history and myth . . . side by side with the historical event of the crucifixion it sets the definitely non-historical event of the resurrection." And yet he went

---

[38]Ibid., 27, 30, 33.

on to ask, "Must we understand it as the cross of Jesus as a figure of past history? Must we go back to the Jesus of history?" And he answered that, although for the first preachers of the gospel that was certainly the case, "for us this personal connection cannot be reproduced."[39]

It should be clear that the only Cross of interest to Bultmann (even as the only Resurrection of interest to him—they form, according to Bultmann, "a single, indivisible cosmic event which brings judgement to the world and opens up for men the possibility of authentic life"[40]) is the *preached* Cross. In a most instructive statement, Bultmann wrote, "The saving efficacy of the cross is not derived from the fact that it is the cross of Christ: it is the cross of Christ because it has this saving efficacy."[41]

Be sure that last statement is clearly understood. Compare it with Ritschl's earlier "value judgment" approach to theological affirmations.

For biblical Christian faith, the saving significance of the cross of Christ lies in the fact that it was the cross of *Christ*. We cannot understand Christ's saving work aright unless we understand something of his person, because Christ's work possesses its unique worth and saving significance for us simply because it is *his* work. The coming into the world of a person, his death, *and, yes, even his resurrection,* would be utterly without saving relevance to my life unless that person were the Messiah, appointed by God as the Second Adam, the New Covenant Head, to save his people from their sins.

Think, for example, of the argument of the letter to the Hebrews. Why is it that the sacrificial death of this One possesses such stupendous significance and is efficacious once for all? It is because he is God's "Son, whom he appointed heir of all things, and through whom he made the universe. The Son is the radiance of God's glory and the exact representation of his being, sustaining all things by his powerful word" (Heb. 1:2–3). This is the One whom the angels worship (1:6) and who is addressed as "God" (1:8), but "who was made a little lower than the angels . . . so that by the grace of God he might taste death for

---

[39]Ibid., 34, 38.
[40]Ibid., 38.
[41]Ibid., 41.

everyone," and who "is not ashamed to call" those whom he makes holy "brothers" and who "shared in their humanity" (2:9, 11, 14).

In other words, the significance of his work is grounded in the significance of his person as the God-man. There have been many crucifixions in history. The Bible makes clear that this Cross possesses a unique character and worth because a unique, divine person died upon it. Read again Philippians 2:6–11.

Bultmann stood this biblical truth on its head. Consider again his statement that "the saving efficacy of the cross is not derived from the fact that it is the cross of Christ," the incarnate Son of God. It is rather the case, according to Bultmann, that we call *this* cross—the Cross with which we are confronted in the preaching of the Christian message— the Cross of "Christ" (the Savior anointed by God), because we have found it to have in our existential experience saving, life-transforming efficacy. "Christ meets us in the preaching as one crucified and risen. . . . The faith of Easter is just this—faith in the word of preaching." It is that kerygma, that preaching, that confronts men "with the question whether they are willing to understand themselves as men who are crucified and risen with Christ."[42] When one recalls Albrecht Ritschl's explanation that such a theological affirmation as the deity of our Lord Jesus Christ is not a metaphysical statement, but rather a value judg- ment,[43] the theological affinity at this point between the liberal Ritschl and the radical Bultmann becomes clear.[44]

Criticism of Bultmann has developed into practically a separate field in theology since he wrote that groundbreaking essay, and in our next chapter we shall be noting the most important forms that criticism has taken within the circle of his disciples. Criticism beyond that circle, obviously, has been even more extensive, and here we can merely take note of some of the most important points that have been emphasized.[45]

---

[42]Ibid.

[43]See chap. 3, sec. 2, above.

[44]"Albrecht Ritschl's 'value-judgments' have come back in a new form, on the basis of a different philosophy" (Althaus, *So-called Kerygma,* 83).

[45]Among the more important conservative Reformed treatments of Bultmann's theology are N. B. Stonehouse, "Rudolf Bultmann's Jesus," in *Paul Before the Areopagus and Other New Testament Studies* (Grand Rapids: Eerdmans, 1957), 109–50; Herman Ridderbos, *Bultmann* (Philadelphia: Presbyterian and Reformed, 1958); and Robert D.

G. N. Stanton devoted a Ph.D. dissertation at Cambridge[46] to demonstrating how, in contrast to later Gnostics who effectively emptied history of its meaning and could virtually dispense with Jesus of Nazareth, the preaching of the early church was characterized by a concern to declare what this Jesus had actually said and done. Stanton and many others have seen in Rudolf Bultmann the marks of a new Gnosticism.

Bultmann's form criticism of the Gospels assumed that there were no eyewitnesses involved in the production of those documents or even on hand to correct them where they may have been in error, or that if such eyewitnesses were alive, they had no interest in the historical accuracy of the gospel traditions. Stanton's thesis speaks to how unlikely that latter notion is, and the dating of the Gospels as early as the sixties by contemporary critics makes the total absence of eyewitnesses extremely unlikely.

We must also challenge Bultmann's insistence that New Testament theology is controlled by the notion of a three-storied universe. Granted the biblical doctrine of inspiration certainly does not imply that the New Testament authors held the scientific concepts taught in our modern universities. But Bultmann caricatures New Testament theology in this regard. He presses an undue literalism upon the writers' language, which fails to take into account what we might speak of as the anthropomorphisms and the phenomenological ("observational") language we find throughout the Scriptures—and commonly use today.[47]

It is not that Bultmann wanted merely to eliminate the New Testament's archaic language. His theology involved a wholesale repudiation of Christian theism, with its doctrines of the eternal, transcendent God and of his creation and providence. What is often spoken of as Bultmann's "scientism," with its concepts of a closed, autonomous universe and man himself as self-contained and autonomous, is viewed as extreme even by some existentialist philosophers.

Knudsen, "Rudolf Bultmann," in *Creative Minds in Contemporary Theology*, ed. Philip E. Hughes (Grand Rapids: Eerdmans, 1969), 131–59.

[46]G. N. Stanton, *Jesus of Nazareth in New Testament Preaching* (Cambridge: Cambridge University Press, 1974).

[47]Ernest Hemingway's title has not been changed from *The Sun Also Rises* to *The Earth Also Revolves!*

And, as already indicated, despite his constant references to the "event" of Christ, Bultmann effectively divorced the Christian gospel from God's redemptive acts *in history* altogether. And thus his demythologization of the New Testament was in reality its dekerygmatization. Bultmann had no saving message left to proclaim.

Yes, the gospel message does contain a strong emphasis on the value of the redemptive event "for us." Think of Romans 6 and Paul's references to *our* dying and being raised with Christ. Or think of Galatians 2:20: "I," the apostle proclaims, "have been crucified with Christ." What we have in such texts, however, is reflection on actual past events and *their* saving significance for the believer. Without the reality of the past event, there is no salvation. Paul emphasizes this crucial point in 1 Corinthians 15: "If Christ has not been raised, our preaching is useless and so is your faith. . . . [Y]ou are still in your sins. Then those also who have fallen asleep in Christ are lost" (vv. 14–18).

In the apostle Paul there is a strong accent on what is sometimes spoken of as "realized eschatology"—the fact that we Christians are those "on whom the fulfillment of the ages has come" (1 Cor. 10:11). God has already "blessed us in the heavenly realms with every spiritual blessing in Christ" (Eph. 1:3). In the total context of Paul's writings, however, this is not to be misunderstood as deeschatologization or as a denial of the consummation yet to come.

8

The Post-Bultmannians

SCHUBERT M. OGDEN wrote his study of *Christ Without Myth* convinced that no theological resource is more significant for moderns than the work of Rudolf Bultmann, "if one considers its capacity for clarifying the problem with which contemporary theology is confronted and for suggesting the lines along which a comprehensive solution may be sought." Nevertheless, Ogden observed that "an emerging consensus" had developed "that Bultmann's solution is inherently inadequate. From responsible voices on practically every side, the claim has come that his theology is structurally inconsistent and therefore open to the most serious criticism."[1]

Ogden himself was one who concluded that Bultmann's proposal "finally fails in being maximally significant because it cannot meet the test of logical self-consistency."[2] He showed how that criticism had been presented both by those who stood to Bultmann's theological "left" and by those who stood to his "right."

---

[1]Schubert M. Ogden, *Christ Without Myth: A Study Based on the Theology of Rudolf Bultmann* (New York: Harper & Brothers, 1961), 18–19, 96.
[2]Ibid., 19.

1. The "Left-wing" Bultmannians: The New Humanism

As we have seen, Bultmann was willing to concede to the historical Jesus of Nazareth virtually no significance for our Christian faith. Affirming the post-Enlightenment principle that historical scholarship can at best produce tentative judgments of probability, Bultmann concluded that Christian faith cannot rest upon the never-certain judgments of the historian. He leaped Lessing's "big ditch" by means of the existential decision of a believing response to the Christian kerygma. He turned the Lutheran (Pauline) affirmation of justification by faith alone in Christ alone—the incarnate Christ who redemptively died and rose again in history—into the affirmation of justification by faith alone in the call to an existential decision alone—the positive, continually-to-be-repeated decision to live an authentic existence of openness to the future. Bultmann insisted that "our ultimate concern is not with historical factuality but with kerygmatic efficacy and existential significance."[3]

Therefore, Bultmann professed no ultimate interest (as contrasted with the merely curious interest of the historian) in *das Was* of Jesus ("what" he said) or *das Wie* of Jesus ("how" he acted). Nevertheless, he continued (for reasons unclear to many) to profess the need to affirm *das Das* of Jesus ("that" he once lived).

It is at this point that some of Bultmann's admirers have criticized him for being too conservative, too orthodox in his theology—a criticism that may seem amazing to evangelical Christians! These critics have insisted that in continuing to speak of the saving act of God in Christ as related somehow to the crucifixion of Jesus of Nazareth, Bultmann failed to present a faith that is totally independent of history. They have therefore accused Bultmann of an ultimate inconsistency and a failure of theological nerve.

In his programmatic 1941 essay, Bultmann himself acknowledged that "anyone who asserts that to speak of an act of God at all is mythological language is bound to regard the idea of an act of God in

---

[3]Ernst Kinder, "Historical Criticism and Demythologizing," in *Kerygma and History,* trans. and ed. Carl E. Braaten and Roy A. Harrisville (New York: Abingdon, 1962), 58.

Christ as a myth."[4] Those whom we are considering here say that this is exactly correct. In maintaining a relation of saving faith to Jesus, in some way or another, Bultmann left the final act of demythologizing unperformed—and they have proceeded to perform it for him!

The message of the New Testament, they claim, is only *one* way—a highly symbolic, mythological way—of expressing the true situation of man—his need to choose authentic existence rather than inauthentic existence. That understanding of the human situation is valid whether or not Jesus ever lived. It is valid even if Jesus of Nazareth himself was merely a myth.

Some of the most important of those who have offered criticism of Bultmann along this line are Karl Jaspers, Fritz Buri, Schubert M. Ogden, and Van Austin Harvey.

Karl Jaspers, the eminent German existentialist who died in 1969, was not a "Bultmannian" at all, but rather a secular philosopher who has been described as "really somewhat on the borderline between the theistic and atheistic thinkers."[5] In 1954, however, Jaspers wrote an essay on "Myth and Religion" that was included by the editor in the second volume of *Kerygma and Myth* as a "welcome voice from the outside."[6]

In that essay, Jaspers accused Bultmann of attempting to provide a new foundation for Christian orthodoxy! Jaspers summarized the enduring debate between "the liberal faith" (using that designation in a very broad sense) and orthodoxy as focusing on this question: "Is man with his reason master and judge of everything that is, can be, and should be, or must he listen to God?" He insisted that Bultmann clearly supported the orthodox answer.[7] According to Jaspers, Jesus should instead be seen as one of many historical examples of authentic existence worthy of emulation. Following Jesus is certainly not the only way to achieve such existence.

---

[4]Rudolf Bultmann et al., *Kerygma and Myth,* ed. Hans Werner Bartsch, rev. trans. Reginald H. Fuller (New York: Harper & Brothers, 1961), 33–34.

[5]Charles C. Anderson, *Critical Quests of Jesus* (Grand Rapids: Eerdmans, 1969), 140.

[6]Hans-Werner Bartsch, ed., *Kerygma and Myth,* vol. 2 (London: SPCK, 1962), vii. In that same volume, the editor defends Bultmann in a chapter entitled "Bultmann and Jaspers," pp. 195–215.

[7]Jaspers, "Myth and Religion," 166–67.

Those who have been labeled the "left-wing Bultmannians"[8] have echoed Jaspers's criticism of their master. Fritz Buri, a professor of theology at the University of Basel, published two volumes of lectures delivered on various university and seminary campuses in the United States during the academic year 1966–67: *Thinking Faith* and *How Can We Still Speak Responsibly of God?*[9] Two earlier series of public lectures presented in Europe were published in English translation as *Theology of Existence*[10] and *Christian Faith in Our Time.*[11] Buri agreed with Bultmann that man experiences authentic human existence through the act of faith: "By accepting our destiny of being that being which in each case has to decide what he will be, we experience the nature of man."[12] He also agreed that "by faith *alone*" means making a sheer personal choice that rests on no objective foundation:

> The more substantial and significant the objects with which it deals, the more important is our decision, and all the more significant the choice for which we must accept the responsibility. Precisely in matters of faith are there decisions for which no objective demonstrations of correctness are possible because the concern is with truth which can be demonstrated only in the open act of concerned involvement.[13]

But Buri disagreed sharply with Bultmann's apparent insistence that saving faith is in some sense faith in Christ. And Bultmann's proposed solution to the problems associated with a faith somehow related to the historical—namely, his insistence that saving faith is faith

---

[8]For example, not only by Ogden (who calls this a "decidedly minority point of view" in *Christ Without Myth,* 98), but also by Van Austin Harvey, *The Historian and the Believer* (New York: Macmillan, 1966), 252. (Harvey revealed his desire to still be considered a Bultmannian by dedicating his book "To Professor Rudolf Bultmann.")

[9]Both volumes were published by Fortress Press (Philadelphia) in 1968.

[10]Fritz Buri, *Theology of Existence,* trans. Harold H. Oliver and Gerhard Onder (Greenwood, S.C.: Attic, 1965).

[11]Fritz Buri, *Christian Faith in Our Time,* trans. Edward Allen Kent (New York: Macmillan, 1966).

[12]Buri, *Thinking Faith,* 28.

[13]Ibid., 88–89.

in the Christ of the kerygma rather than in the Christ of history—was deemed by Buri to be no solution at all:

> This character of the givenness of all achievement in the actualization of our destiny to responsible personhood is precisely what is meant in the New Testament message of Christ the Redeemer. . . . This event, however, is not bound up with either Jesus or the mythology of the Christ. It occurs wherever man understands himself as absolutely responsible and experiences the fulfillment of his destiny. However powerful historically the Christian ideas and concepts have become for this redeeming self-understanding, its content is not bound to these historical forms. . . . Why should it be that only Christianity should know about the genuine nature of man as a person summoned to grace? . . .
>
> . . . The kingdom of God occurs wherever man knows himself to be absolutely responsible for another in personal community and wherever he attempts to form his world from this attachment.[14]

In the United States, the impact of Buri's program for an allegedly "Christian natural theology"[15] has been especially strong in schools associated with the United Methodist Church. During his academic year in the United States, Buri was guest professor at Drew University. His English translator, Harold H. Oliver, was a professor at Boston University. Schubert M. Ogden and Van Austin Harvey, who were perhaps the two leading American proponents of a similar theological position, were once colleagues at Perkins School of Theology at Southern Methodist University. And although Buri distanced himself from the specifically process metaphysics of John B. Cobb, Jr., of the School of Theology at Claremont, he also recognized the affinities between their positions.[16]

Near the end of the previous chapter, I accused Bultmann of effectively eliminating the saving message from the New Testament altogether. Since that message is the good news of God's redemptive acts in Christ in history, his program of demythologizing the New

---

[14]Ibid., 91, 100.
[15]Buri, *How Can We Still Speak?* 58.
[16]Buri, *Thinking Faith,* vii.

Testament was in reality the dekerygmatization of the New Testament. Schubert Ogden has noted with appreciation Buri's insistence that dekerygmatization of a more thorough nature than that achieved by Bultmann is precisely what is needed if we are to move beyond Bultmann to the truth:

> The only tenable alternative to Bultmann's position, therefore, is to reject his appeal to a mythological saving-event as incompatible with modern man's picture of himself and his world and, in so doing, to carry to its logical conclusion, to the point of "dekerygmatization," the program of demythologization he proposes.[17]

Ogden insisted that any theology continues to be mythological, and therefore untenable, "to the extent to which it denies that statements about God may be interpreted as statements about man."[18]

Ogden himself praised Bultmann for making it clear that "so far as its content is concerned, Christian faith is nothing other than that freedom from the past and openness for the future that is the original possibility of authentic human existence."[19] But Ogden criticized Bultmann severely that "for all of Bultmann's emphasis on unlimited demythologization, he is equally insistent that it is because of the event of Jesus of Nazareth *and it alone* that Christian faith or authentic historical existence is factually possible."[20]

The ultimate failure of Bultmann's reinterpretation of New Testament theology, Ogden insisted, lies in the fact

> that not both of these propositions can be true, since when they are taken together they involve a logical self-contradiction. If, as the first proposition affirms, Christian faith is to be interpreted solely in existential terms as man's original possibility of authentic self-understanding, then it demonstrably follows that it must be independent of any particular historical occurrence. On the other hand, if the second proposition is true and Christian faith has a necessary connection with a particular event,

---

[17]Ogden, *Christ Without Myth*, 110.
[18]Ibid., 137.
[19]Ibid., 113.
[20]Ibid., 117 (Ogden's italics).

then clearly it may not be interpreted without remainder as man's original possibility of authentic historicity.[21]

Is authentic existence a possibility open to man as such, or is authentic existence a possibility open to man only because of a particular historical event—the historical life of Jesus of Nazareth, however much or however little one thinks one can know about that life? Bultmann wanted to have it both ways, according to Ogden, and that cannot be. The Augustinian (Calvinist) might observe that Ogden is guilty of the Pelagian error of thinking that ability limits responsibility,[22] but it would be ironic indeed for Bultmann to seek refuge in a biblically Reformed anthropology.

Like Buri, but in contrast to Bultmann, Ogden insisted that "the only final condition for sharing in authentic life that the New Testament lays down is a condition that can be formulated in complete abstraction from the event Jesus of Nazareth and all that it specifically imports."[23] If the church is to present to the world "a genuinely postliberal theology," it must be a theology in which the Christian faith is "interpreted exhaustively and without remainder as man's original possibility of authentic existence as this is clarified and conceptualized by an appropriate philosophical analysis."[24]

Where Ogden went beyond Buri was in suggesting that that "appropriate philosophical analysis" would not be based exclusively on a Heideggerian existentialism, but would also make use of the insights of process philosophy, "especially as developed by Charles Hartshorne."[25]

Bultmann's vigorous antisupernaturalism and his radical skepticism with regard to the historical value of the Gospels clearly left him vulnerable to the criticism that he arbitrarily short-circuited his program of demythologizing and existentializing the New Testament message by continuing to speak of a unique saving act of God in Christ.

---

[21]Ogden, *Christ Without Myth,* 117.

[22]Ogden stated that principle in its Kantian form: *"Du kannst, denn du sollst* ['You can, because you should']" (*Christ Without Myth,* 118).

[23]Ibid., 143.

[24]Ibid., 146.

[25]Ibid., 151.

Indeed, Bultmann would seem to be able to offer no cogent answer to this criticism.

2. The "Right-wing" Bultmannians: The New Quest

The terms *left-wing* and *right-wing* are, of course, quite general, often ambiguous, and therefore not always very helpful. Bultmann proposed such a radical departure from orthodox Christian faith that he left quite a bit of room to his "right"! To lump together all those who stand to Bultmann's right does not get us very far. Schubert Ogden has commented on the fact that critics to the right of Bultmann range all the way from those who seem to be quite close to Bultmann himself (such as John Macquarrie and Emil Brunner) to those who wish to distance themselves very far indeed from Bultmann, like the conservative Lutheran theologians Ernst Kinder and Walter Künneth, and most of the Roman Catholics. Ogden himself singles out Karl Barth as the theologian to Bultmann's right most worthy of attention.[26] Charles Anderson, in his chapter entitled "Critics to the Right of Bultmann," discusses Ethelbert Stauffer, Joachim Jeremias, and Walter Künneth.[27] By that token, however, many other "moderate" New Testament scholars of our time might well be considered, such as Oscar Cullmann or Vincent Taylor, or even those much more conservative Reformed critics of Bultmann, Ned Stonehouse and Herman Ridderbos, referred to in footnote 45 to the previous chapter.

In the first section of this chapter, we discussed those who may be considered left-wing Bultmannians. In like manner, we will now consider the right-wing Bultmannians (not all of the critics on his right)—that is, those who have definitely seen themselves as disciples of Bultmann, but who have wanted to "pull back" from the master, as we shall see, at one particular point.[28]

---

[26]Ibid., especially 97–105. See Barth's vigorous criticism of Bultmann in "Rudolf Bultmann—An Attempt to Understand Him," in Bartsch, *Kerygma and Myth*, 2:83–132.

[27]Anderson, *Critical Quests of Jesus,* 121–39.

[28]Those whom we shall mention now are discussed by Anderson in his chapter entitled "Critics Within the Circle of Bultmann: The New Quest," in *Critical Quests of Jesus,* 155–200.

These right-wing Bultmannians were uneasy with Bultmann's notion that Christian faith could be content to know nothing of significance about the Jesus of history beyond the fact that he really lived. Therefore, they embarked on what has been designated the "New Quest" of the historical Jesus.[29] Its proponents had a far more modest goal, however, than that which impelled the original quest. They had imbibed too much of Bultmann's form-critical skepticism to think that they could ever produce anything like a life of Jesus. They were challenged, however, by this question: If the heart of the Christian kerygma of the crucified and risen Jesus Christ is the good news that by the existential decision of faith one may know authentic existence— "the abandonment of all self-contrived security,"[30] trust in God, openness to the future—then is it not important to know whether that historical person whose life somehow "triggered" that faith and that message himself personally knew such authentic existence, such trust in the grace of God, such openness to the future? The only alternative to a positive answer to that question would seem to be the position of such thinkers as Jaspers, Buri, and Ogden (see section 1, above), namely, the insistence that the only important thing is whether *I* know such an authentic, existential attitude toward life—whether Jesus ever did or not!

The "New Questers" were Bultmannians. They were not willing to follow the path of the Bultmannian left. But neither were they totally satisfied with the position of their teacher. Contrary to Bultmann himself, they believed that in order to affirm that the saving message is the message concerning Jesus Christ, one must know that the historical Jesus himself had an authentic human existence. The "modest proposal" of the New Quest was that the gospel records should be reexamined to see whether this can be shown.

The goal of the Old Quest had been to discover as much as possible about the historical Jesus, and historians differed widely as to how much could be discovered. In many cases, however, what was considered ascertainable was a great deal indeed. Those who

---

[29]Note the title of the survey by James M. Robinson, which remains the best treatment of this phenomenon: *A New Quest of the Historical Jesus* (London: SCM, 1959).

[30]Bultmann, *Kerygma and Myth,* 19.

set forth on the New Quest had a much more limited aim, as they saw it: not to trace Jesus' life, but at least to determine his existential self-understanding.

There have been many studies of the so-called new quest of the historical Jesus. Too often, however, the real goal of the quest has not been made clear.[31] This is unfortunate, because the New Quest cannot be properly understood without understanding its motivation. Only then can one see what made that quest "tick," and only then will one not miss the forest for the trees. Some exponents of the New Quest studied those sayings of Jesus *(das Was)* which the form critics considered probably authentic (because they fulfill the criterion of dissimilarity[32]), and others studied his supposedly probable conduct *(das Wie)*. But in both cases their basic aim was to establish that authentic existence is not only available today to the one who responds in faith to the message about Jesus, but was also experienced by that historical Jesus himself.

Concentrating upon the authentic sayings of Jesus were Ernst Käsemann of Tübingen, whose 1953 lecture is generally recognized as the inauguration of the New Quest,[33] Gerhard Ebeling of Zurich,[34] and Günther Bornkamm of Heidelberg.[35] Bornkamm stressed how Jesus, in his teaching (which he presented with such remarkable, unprecedented authority), brought men and women face-to-face with the unmediated presence of God and thus with the necessity of making an eschatological, existential decision. Jesus' conduct received attention from Ernst Fuchs of Berlin.[36] Fuchs emphasized Jesus' readiness to have fellowship with tax collectors and sinners, and his conscious decision to follow the path of John as a preacher of the kingdom, even though he knew that to be

---

[31]See, for example, the otherwise helpful survey by Ha-bae Kan [Harvie Conn], "The New Quest for the Historical Jesus," *Themelios* 6, no. 2 (1969): 25–40.

[32]This criterion was discussed in chap. 7, sec. 1, above.

[33]Ernst Käsemann, "The Problem of the Historical Jesus," in *Essays on New Testament Themes,* trans. W. J. Montague (London: SCM, 1964), 15–47.

[34]Gerhard Ebeling, *Word and Faith,* trans. James W. Leitch (Philadelphia: Fortress, 1963).

[35]Günther Bornkamm, *Jesus of Nazareth,* trans. Irene and Fraser McLuskey (New York: Harper and Row, 1960).

[36]Ernst Fuchs, *Studies of the Historical Jesus* (London: SCM, 1964).

such a preacher was to invite execution. These four members of the so-called Marburg School (the label indicating that they had all studied under Bultmann at Marburg)—Käsemann, Bornkamm, Ebeling, and Fuchs—have been recognized as the most significant pioneers in the New Quest.

The basic problem for the New Quest, however, is that its goal is not nearly so "modest" as its proponents seem to think it is. As we have already noted, the advocates of the New Quest have stressed that their concern to discover Jesus' existential self-understanding must not be confused with the liberal desire to discover his psychological self-consciousness and perhaps even trace its development during his ministry. Norman Perrin explains that one's self-understanding "means the understanding of the self's own existence, but, at the same time, it does not mean the process of experience, reflection, decision, and so on, by means of which that understanding is reached; that would be self-consciousness."[37]

This distinction, however, is not as clear to many of the New Quest's critics as it is to its supporters. (Perrin himself acknowledges that "it is difficult to grasp."[38]) And whatever the real significance of the distinction may be, it can hardly be denied that were we to know what the historical Jesus' existential self-understanding was, we would know a great deal about him—much more than the skeptical form-critical methodology of these Bultmannians would seem to allow.[39]

James Robinson, for example, defined authentic existence as "selfhood constituted by commitment," an existence that "consists in constant *engagement.*" Therefore, "selfhood . . . is to be understood only . . . by laying hold of the understanding of existence in terms of which the self is constituted." Robinson was confident that this exis-

---

[37]Norman Perrin, *Rediscovering the Teaching of Jesus* (New York: Harper & Row, 1967), 223.

[38]Ibid., 222–23.

[39]Ben F. Meyer reminds us that the Old Quest "came to grief . . . not for merely technical reasons. The seeds of failure were sown at a deeper level, in the presuppositions of the historians. The 'old mistake' lay in these presuppositions. Furthermore, it remains a question whether 'the old mistake' was not continued in the presuppositions of what came to be called 'the new quest'. The fruitful area of discussion and debate, then, is the area of presuppositions" (*The Aims of Jesus* [London: SCM, 1979], 14).

tentialist perspective on the self, as known in terms of its "commitment" and "intention," distanced the New Quest from the
"psychologism" of the Old Quest and presented the scholar with a
proper subject for research with regard to the Jesus of history: "Jesus'
understanding of his existence, his self-hood, and thus in the higher
sense his life, is a possible subject of historical research."[40]

Such an argument, however, seems unlikely to convince those
outside the New Quest camp.[41] The left-wing Bultmannians have certainly not been impressed with it. In a chapter entitled "How New Is
the 'New Quest of the Historical Jesus'?" Van A. Harvey and Schubert
M. Ogden asked: "Is the new quest for the *existentiell* selfhood of Jesus
different from the old quest for the 'inner life' of Jesus, his 'personality'? And if it is impossible to recover Jesus' 'inner life'—as Robinson
claims—is it any easier to recover Jesus' *existentiell* selfhood?"[42]

Early in this century, Albert Schweitzer tellingly criticized the
Old Quest for its obvious subjectivity, noting how each searcher for the
real Jesus had found a Jesus who very closely resembled the searcher
himself in terms of his philosophy and/or theology. Precisely the same
criticism is in order when we examine the New Quest. Once we
recognize what these existentialist theologians have been looking for
in the Gospels—namely, a Jesus who had experienced in a unique way
the authentic existence praised by Heideggerian philosophy—we are
not greatly surprised to learn that they have found him.

3. Redaction Criticism

When considering the extraordinary significance of Rudolf Bultmann,[43]
we noted that he was a seminal thinker with regard to both New
Testament critical methodology and New Testament theology. In the

---

[40]Robinson, *New Quest,* 46, 68, 72.

[41]For Bultmann's own criticism of the New Quest, see his "The Primitive Christian
Kerygma and the Historical Jesus," in *The Historical Jesus and the Kerygmatic Christ,*
trans. and ed. Carl E. Braaten and Roy A. Harrisville (New York: Abingdon, 1964),
15–42.

[42]In Braaten and Harrisville, *Historical Jesus,* 234.

[43]In chap. 7, above.

first two sections of this chapter, we have been looking primarily at the theological concerns of Bultmann's most significant disciples. There has also been, however, a major new development with regard to the methodology of Gospels study since Bultmann, and to this we now turn.

In the first section of chapter 3, we surveyed the development of source criticism in the nineteenth century. In chapter 7, we examined the methodology of form criticism, which was introduced early in the twentieth century. To these there was added, in the years immediately following the Second World War, what has come to be referred to as redaction criticism.[44] For the most part, these three disciplines may be viewed as mutually complementary, consecutive stages in Gospels criticism.

First, the critic reaches certain conclusions about the literary relationship among our extant gospels (especially among the three synoptics). Most scholars continue to hold that source criticism has established that Mark was the earliest of our canonical gospels, and that Matthew and Luke were composed using Mark, Q (a lost collection of Jesus' sayings), and additional material distinctive of the particular gospel in question (Matthew or Luke).

Second, the critic seeks to examine the oral tradition that lay behind those written sources, consisting of individual, isolated units— both stories and sayings. Using the principles of form criticism, the critic believes he can reconstruct the original form of these units and group them according to their style (genre) and the *Sitz im Leben* in the early church that would have given rise to them.

Third, redaction criticism comes into play. The critic looks at each gospel again as a unified whole, as a finished product. Since he has discerned (he believes) what elements came from the tradition (the written tradition of Mark and Q, and behind them the original oral tradition), the critic can now determine how each Evangelist made use

---

[44]It was Willi Marxsen who first proposed *Redaktionsgeschichte* as the label for this discipline, in the first edition of *Der Evangelist Markus* (Göttingen: Vandenhoeck & Ruprecht, 1956). See his *Mark the Evangelist,* trans. James Boyce et al. (Nashville: Abingdon, 1969), 21. In that volume *Redaktionsgeschichte* was translated "redaction history," but "redaction criticism" has become the standard translation, even as "form criticism" has become the accepted rendering of *Formgeschichte.*

of that tradition in order to present the theological message that he wanted to convey. In speaking of "how each Evangelist made use of that tradition," we refer to all the means any writer uses in order to produce a written document: choosing what to include and what to omit from his sources, arranging the material in a certain order, modifying in some way the stories and sayings available in the tradition, as well as creating new material not found in any of the writer's sources. Therefore, redaction criticism involves not only "redaction" in the narrow sense of "editing," but more broadly "composition" as well.

Redaction criticism, emphasizing the distinctive theology of each gospel, could not have arisen until source criticism and form criticism had made it possible (so it is assumed) to separate out (1) the original gospel elements in their original (oral) form, (2) those elements as they were collected in Q, and (3) those elements as they were put together by Mark. One must be able to see what was Luke's own contribution to his gospel, so to speak, or Matthew's to his, or Mark's to his (though determining Mark's contribution may appear to be the most difficult task), if one is to discover the particular theological concern of each Evangelist.

Thus we may speak of the complementary character of these three forms of Gospels criticism: source criticism, form criticism, and redaction criticism. It is also true, however, that redaction critics have emphasized certain differences between their method and the previous kinds of criticism, at least as previously practiced.

For example, with regard to earlier source criticism, Norman Perrin has said that "the starting point for redaction criticism" is the rejection of the once-popular Marcan hypothesis—not the view that Mark is the earliest of our gospels (that is still accepted), but "the assumption that, as the earliest, it (Mark) is a reliable historical source."[45] For this reason, as we have seen,[46] William Wrede is credited with being the "father" of redaction criticism. He was the first to insist that Mark had a theological "ax to grind" in his gospel and that what appeared to be historical reporting was often literary device employed to serve that theological purpose.

---

[45]Norman Perrin, *What Is Redaction Criticism?* (Philadelphia: Fortress, 1969), 7.
[46]In chap. 4, sec. 1.

With regard to form criticism, Willi Marxsen, in his influential *Mark the Evangelist,* devoted a fifteen-page introduction to a presentation of the differences between redaction criticism and the earlier form criticism.[47] He pointed to three primary differences:

1. The form critics viewed the Evangelists as little more than compilers or editors. Dibelius's remark was "typical": "The composers are only to the smallest extent authors. They are principally collectors, vehicles of tradition, editors."[48] The redaction critic, on the other hand, views the Evangelists as truly authors, as creative literary figures: "As far as we can tell, Mark is the first to bring the individualistic element to the forming and shaping of the tradition."[49]

2. The form critic was concerned with the smallest units of tradition and their origin. The redaction critic is concerned with the grouping of the various small units into larger units, and his ultimate concern is with the total unit, the finished gospel. Thus, the redaction critic raises the question of how the gospel genre arose in the first place, and then addresses the questions of *how* and *why* each particular gospel was put together as it was.

3. The form critic was concerned with the church's *Sitz im Leben Kirche,* that is, the life-situation in the early church—the communal setting and needs—that gave birth to the gospel tradition. And some of the more conservative form critics have sought to determine at certain points in the tradition the earlier *Sitz im Leben Jesu,* "an actual situation of the life of Jesus" himself in which a saying was uttered.[50] The redaction critic does not ignore these life-situations—at least not the life-situation in the primitive church. (In actual practice, redaction criticism has given little attention to the life-situation of Jesus himself.) It is the distinctive concern of redaction criticism, however, to focus on what Marxsen referred to as the "*third* situation-in-life":[51] the *Sitz im Leben* of the Evangelist, the particular theological purposes of the individual gospel author himself. According to Marxsen: "With this

---

[47]Marxsen, *Mark the Evangelist,* 15–29.

[48]Quoted by Marxsen, *Mark the Evangelist,* 15.

[49]Ibid., 19.

[50]Joachim Jeremias, *The Parables of Jesus,* 3d rev. ed., trans. S. H. Hooke (London: SCM, 1972), 21.

[51]Marxsen, *Mark the Evangelist,* 23 (Marxsen's italics).

approach, the question as to what really happened is excluded from the outset. We inquire rather how the evangelists describe what happened."[52]

Thus, while Marxsen could acknowledge that redaction criticism "can . . . learn much from work previously done," and could even speak of "the great similarity between redaction history and form history," his emphasis was on the fact that "their similarity ought not deceive us as to their differences." Indeed, so little did he see redaction criticism building on the work of form criticism that he suggested that, "theoretically, it would have been possible for redaction-historical research to have begun immediately after literary criticism. It is really quite astonishing that it did not."[53] After all, Wrede antedated Bultmann. But, as a matter of fact, redaction criticism did not begin in earnest until after the Second World War.

Although Norman Perrin praised the 1934 Bampton Lectures of R. H. Lightfoot[54] as "an altogether remarkable work" and suggested that "Lightfoot was actually the first redaction critic," Perrin himself well described what he called "the flowering of the discipline":

> Just as three scholars emerged with independent works marking the beginning of form criticism proper after the hiatus caused by the First World War,[55] so three scholars came forward with independent works denoting the beginning of redaction criticism proper after the hiatus caused by the Second World War.[56]

Those three scholars were Günther Bornkamm,[57] Hans Conzelmann, and Willi Marxsen. Each has concentrated on the study of a different synoptic gospel: Bornkamm on Matthew, Conzelmann on Luke, and Marxsen on Mark.

---

[52]Ibid., 23–24.

[53]Ibid., 21–22.

[54]Robert Henry Lightfoot, *History and Interpretation in the Gospels* (London: Hodder and Stoughton, 1935).

[55]Namely, Karl Ludwig Schmidt, Martin Dibelius, and Rudolf Bultmann; see chap. 7, sec. 1, above.

[56]Perrin, *What Is Redaction Criticism?* 25.

[57]Reference has already been made to Günther Bornkamm in section 2 of this chapter, since he has also been important in the New Quest of the historical Jesus.

In *Mark the Evangelist* (which first appeared in German in 1956), Marxsen concluded that the Gospel of Mark was written between A.D. 66 and 70, after the Christian community had fled into the mountains of Galilee at the beginning of the Jewish War, there to await the imminent Parousia of the Lord. The apparent prophecy of Mark 13:14 ("When you see 'the abomination that causes desolation' standing where it does not belong—let the reader understand—then let those who are in Judea flee to the mountains") was actually written after this flight from the holy city of Jerusalem had already taken place. The references in Mark 14:28 and 16:7 to Christ's meeting the disciples in Galilee are not references to Christ's post-Resurrection appearances, but rather to the Parousia, which Mark the Evangelist anticipated taking place very soon.[58]

Bornkamm's first two published studies of Matthew's Gospel appeared in German in 1948 and 1954 and in English translation in 1963.[59] In the first study, he treated the pericope of the stilling of the storm (Matt. 8:23–27) "as an example for making clear the evangelist's method of working." He sought to show how Matthew has taken what appears in Mark as "a straightforward miracle story" and, by placing it in a different context and introducing it with the reference to Jesus' disciples "following" him (v. 23), has made the story a theological and "kerygmatic paradigm of the danger and glory of discipleship."[60]

Bornkamm's second essay is again brief, but it is a rather comprehensive study of the principal themes that are distinctive of Matthew's theology: his eschatology, his Christology, his view of the relation between Jesus and the Law, and his ecclesiology.[61]

Perrin has said that "if Günther Bornkamm is the first of the true redaction critics, Hans Conzelmann is certainly the most important."[62]

---

[58]Marxsen, *Mark the Evangelist,* 75, 85, 171, 182–88.

[59]Günther Bornkamm, Gerhard Barth, and Heinz Joachim Held, *Tradition and Interpretation in Matthew,* trans. Percy Scott (Philadelphia: Westminster, 1963).

[60]Bornkamm, "The Stilling of the Storm in Matthew," in Bornkamm et al., *Tradition and Interpretation in Matthew,* 53, 57.

[61]Bornkamm, "End-expectation and Church in Matthew," in Bornkamm et al., *Tradition and Interpretation in Matthew,* 15–51.

[62]Perrin, *What Is Redaction Criticism?* 28–29.

Before Conzelmann, Luke had been viewed as a great historian. After Conzelmann, Luke has come to be seen as a great theologian.

According to Conzelmann, the "problem" with which Luke was concerned was the "delay" (the nonoccurrence) of the Parousia, which the church had been anticipating as imminent. Luke's solution was to replace the earlier two-foci (promise and fulfillment) understanding of the history of salvation with a new, three-foci structure in which the ministry of Jesus is viewed, not as the end-time event, but rather as the central or mid-time event in a history that moves from the time of Israel to the time of Jesus to the time of the church.

Conzelmann considered Luke 16:16 to be a key text for understanding Luke's new theological reading of salvation history: "The Law and the Prophets were proclaimed until John. Since that time, the good news of the kingdom of God is being preached, and everyone is forcing his way into it." Thus, McKnight summarizes, it was in the writings of Luke

> that the distinction between the period of Jesus and the period of the church becomes fully conscious. . . . This defines the Christology and ecclesiology of Luke and causes him to transform eschatology into a broad scheme of the history of salvation. . . . Luke's reaction to the delay of the parousia resulted in a reconstruction so radical that a timeless message was resounded and the length of the interim period no longer constituted a problem.[63]

A comparison of Luke and his sources (primarily Mark) demonstrates, according to Conzelmann, "that it is not an adequate explanation of Luke's alterations to see them merely as 'development', but that it is a question of a definite theological attitude to the problem of eschatology. Luke in fact replaces the early expectation by a comprehensive scheme of a different kind."[64] We are reminded of F. C. Baur's

---

[63]Edgar V. McKnight, "Form and Redaction Criticism," in *The New Testament and Its Modern Interpreters,* ed. Eldon Jay Epp and George W. MacRae (Atlanta: Scholars Press, 1989), 154.

[64]Hans Conzelmann, *The Theology of St Luke,* trans. Geoffrey Buswell (New York: Harper & Brothers, 1960), 96. This work was originally published as *Die Mitte der Zeit: Studien zur Theologie des Lukas* (Tübingen: J. C. B. Mohr, 1953).

emphasis on the all-controlling *Tendenz* of each of the New Testament writers.[65]

Writing in 1969, Norman Perrin expressed the judgment that Conzelmann's *The Theology of St Luke* "ranks with Bultmann's *History of the Synoptic Tradition* . . . as one of the few truly seminal works of our time in the field of New Testament research."[66] And yet, just six years later, Ward Gasque noted that "there is no general agreement among scholars on even the most basic issues of Lucan research."[67] And Charles H. Talbert, writing the next year, concluded that "although overstated," Gasque's assertion is generally true:

> Lucan studies in the last twenty years have been like shifting sands. At present, widespread agreement is difficult to find, except on the point that Conzelmann's synthesis is inadequate. Until the scholarly community can agree on a proper procedure for studying Luke-Acts, there is little likelihood that another synthesis will fare any better.[68]

An updated form of Talbert's article appears as chapter 11 in *The New Testament and Its Modern Interpreters*.[69] It is a detailed and helpful review of Lucan studies since the "new look" in such studies emerged in Germany after 1950, showing how virtually every major conclusion reached by Conzelmann has now been seriously questioned. Talbert declares, "Most devastating to Conzelmann's reconstruction is the fact that subsequent scholars have been able to interpret the Lucan effort to write in terms of salvation history as due to a number of different occasions other than a delayed parousia."[70]

Marshall, for example, is one who has recently emphasized that the case for seeing a sharp contrast between Mark's theology and Luke's has not been made: "For Luke what Mark recorded was, as

---

[65]See chap. 2, sec. 3, above.

[66]Perrin, *What Is Redaction Criticism?* 29.

[67]Ward Gasque, *A History of the Criticism of the Acts of the Apostles* (Tübingen: J. C. B. Mohr, 1975), 305.

[68]Charles H. Talbert, "Shifting Sands: The Recent Study of the Gospel of Luke," *Interpretation* 30 (October 1976): 395.

[69]Talbert, "Luke-Acts," in *The New Testament,* ed. Epp and MacRae, 297–320.

[70]Ibid., 301.

Mark had said, only the beginning, and Luke desired to present the full story. Although Mark himself had not taken this step, what he did was in principle open to expansion." Marshall insists that "in principle the attempt to detect elaborate theological motivation behind every piece of Lucan redaction is wrongheaded, and we should pay more attention perhaps to Luke as a literary stylist."[71]

Soon after the publication of the English translation of Conzelmann's study, Ned B. Stonehouse pointed out that "Conzelmann himself makes no attempt to establish his view" that the "delay of the parousia" was a grave problem seriously disturbing the faith of the early church. Conzelmann simply presupposes this.[72]

The subjective nature of every attempt to find just one overriding theological "occasion" or "tendency" that will explain all the distinctives of the Luke-Acts record has become increasingly evident. Talbert believes that

> redaction criticism has been unable to delineate either the Lucan purpose or the Lucan *Sitz im Leben*. . . . In sum, redaction criticism has enabled us to see the author as a creative theologian with a perspective of his own and to discern parts of that point of view. It has not enabled us to grasp Luke's purpose in the context of his *Sitz im Leben*.[73]

Redaction criticism asked us to choose between reading Luke as a historian or recognizing him to be a theologian. Talbert notes that while redaction criticism has resulted in "a new appreciation of Luke as a theologian alongside Paul and John," at the same time "a protest has been heard" in recent years "against current historical skepticism."[74]

In evaluating redaction criticism as an interpretive method, it is well to remember that Bible-believing Christians have always considered it legitimate, and important, to seek to discern the particular

---

[71]I. Howard Marshall, "Luke and His 'Gospel,'" in *The Gospel and the Gospels,* ed. Peter Stuhlmacher (Grand Rapids: Eerdmans, 1991), 278, 290.

[72]Ned B. Stonehouse, review of *The Theology of St Luke,* by Hans Conzelmann, *Westminster Theological Journal* 24 (November 1961): 67.

[73]Talbert, "Luke-Acts," 305.

[74]Ibid., 311.

perspective of each gospel writer and the major emphases in each gospel. Indeed, in our preaching we cannot do full justice to a passage unless we realize that its context extends broadly to that entire gospel with its distinctive emphases. I recall how struck I was years ago as a first-year student at Westminster Seminary when Professor Edmund Clowney insisted that a sermon on a particular event in Jesus' ministry would be a quite different sermon depending on which of the gospels the text had been chosen from.

Redaction criticism is, therefore, an approach with which an orthodox Christian can have more sympathy—and therefore one in which he or she can have more interest—than the earlier form criticism, which claimed to be able to break apart the gospel "string" and examine each individual "pearl" meaningfully without regard to that string. The orthodox believer has resisted the form-critical methodology because he knows that the Holy Spirit has not given us so many individual literary pearls, but rather four beautifully strung necklaces, if you will. Because redaction criticism's primary concern has been with each gospel as a finished product, many orthodox Christians have been ready to learn new insights from it.

Indeed, my New Testament professor at Westminster a generation ago, Ned B. Stonehouse, may be viewed as one who was ahead of his time in anticipating some of the primary emphases of redaction criticism.[75] Moisés Silva has noted, however, that it would be quite misleading to call Stonehouse a "redaction critic" as that label is normally understood.[76] Indeed, "while redaction criticism was formed

---

[75]Grant R. Osborne, for example, lists Stonehouse along with Wrede and R. H. Lightfoot as "several precursors to Redaction Criticism" ("Redaction Criticism," in *New Testament Criticism and Interpretation,* ed. David Alan Black and David S. Dockery [Grand Rapids: Zondervan, 1991], 201).

See especially Ned B. Stonehouse, *The Witness of Matthew and Mark to Christ* (Philadelphia: Presbyterian Guardian, 1944), and *The Witness of Luke to Christ* (Grand Rapids: Eerdmans, 1951). These two books were later published in one volume, *The Witness of the Synoptic Gospels to Christ* (Grand Rapids: Baker, 1979).

For a study of this aspect of Stonehouse's teaching, see especially Moisés Silva, "Ned B. Stonehouse and Redaction Criticism," *Westminster Theological Journal* 40 (Fall 1977): 77–88; 40 (Spring 1978): 281–303.

[76]Silva, "Stonehouse and Redaction Criticism," 282.

in the womb of historical scepticism of the most severe kind, Stonehouse's work was designed to strengthen confidence in the historical reliability of the gospels!"[77]

Nevertheless, in his preface to *The Witness of Luke to Christ,* Stonehouse wrote this:

> In particular it has seemed to me that Christians who are assured as to the unity of the witness of the Gospels should take greater pains to do justice to the diversity of expression of that witness. It is a thrilling experience to observe this unity, to be overwhelmed at the contemplation of the *one* Christ proclaimed by the four evangelists. But that experience is far richer and more satisfying if one has been absorbed and captured by each portrait in turn and has conscientiously been concerned with the minutest differentiating details as well as with the total impact of the evangelical witness.[78]

Stonehouse wanted the student of the Gospels continually to keep in mind the question, Why has God by the inspiration of his Spirit given us not one but four gospels? Regard for the distinctive elements of each gospel, and for each paragraph of each gospel, as significant parts of the whole New Testament witness to Christ, is the rightful heritage of orthodox Christian scholarship. Justice must be done both to the unity of the Gospels (their common proclamation of the coming of the King and his kingdom) and to their diversity (the distinctive portraits painted by the Evangelists under the control of the Holy Spirit).

Thus, the evangelical believer can appreciate redaction criticism's emphasis on the unifying integrity and the distinctiveness of each of the gospels. But, as we have stressed again and again in this survey, the Christian must never lose sight of the crucial importance of the presuppositions with which the critic operates. The major redaction critics have approached their study with the assumption that the Bible is just like any other collection of books. It is certainly not infallible, or even historically reliable, in their opinion.

And, of course, as we have seen, redaction criticism itself depends heavily on supposedly being able to view the individual units of

---

[77]Ibid., 78.
[78]Stonehouse, *Witness of Luke,* 6.

the gospel tradition in their original form before they were combined by the Evangelists. The work of redaction criticism also rests upon the assumed ability to identify the earlier form of the tradition by the methods of literary and form criticism. Redaction criticism is thus an upper-story structure that rests upon a most questionable foundation. Remember that the entire critical enterprise so hangs together that it is only as strong as its weakest link.

Redaction criticism as a "science" was created by scholars who did not believe the gospel writers were "carried along by the Holy Spirit" (2 Peter 1:21) and thus produced inerrant Scripture, which is the Word of God written. Therefore, these scholars have been open to the possibility not only that there may be contradictions and errors in the Gospels, but also that events and sayings were "made up out of whole cloth," as we say. Indeed, they have assumed from the beginning of their studies that such *will* be found in the Gospels.[79]

Stonehouse reminded us that it has been a significant emphasis of redaction criticism to charge the Evangelists "with having substantially and tendentiously rewritten their sources in the interest of producing Gospels articulating their own individual historical and theological points of view as they had developed in the course of time."[80] The assumption that certain parts of the Gospels were actually *created* by the Evangelists must be challenged on at least two grounds:

1. The question must be squarely faced: does this not involve the Evangelists in deception?[81] Like many others, Norman Perrin tries to assure us that the ancients had a concept of historical writing totally

---

[79]I am reminded of F. W. Beare's statement at the beginning of a Ph.D. course on "The Death of Christ," in which I had enrolled at Trinity College, University of Toronto, that "in this course we shall all assume not merely that there *may* be conflicting views of the meaning of Christ's death among the various New Testament writers, but that there surely *will* be." In context, that statement was not simply an assertion of a conclusion to which Beare's studies of the New Testament had empirically brought him, but was rather the presupposition he viewed as required by a recognition that the New Testament writings are exclusively human—and thus not inerrant or infallible.

[80]Ned B. Stonehouse, *Origins of the Synoptic Gospels* (Grand Rapids: Eerdmans, 1963), 111–12.

[81]In an examination of *Tendenzkritik,* C. F. D. Moule has written: "And here I feel bound to bring up a consideration that is unpopular with critics, namely, the moral

different from ours, but classical historians would question that conten-
tion. Certainly Perrin's insistence that "the early church . . . saw no
reason to distinguish between words originally spoken by the historical
Jesus bar Joseph from Nazareth and words ascribed to him in the
tradition of the church"[82] flies in the face of the apostle Paul's careful
distinction in 1 Corinthians 7 between what he, the apostle, says and
what the Lord himself said. He made this distinction even though he
regarded both the teaching of Jesus and his own teaching as authoritative (study vv. 10–12 and 40). And Perrin's definition of a "gospel"
as "a strange mixture of history, legend, and myth"[83] is certainly not the
apostle Peter's definition. Note Peter's clear rejection of *mythois* in 2
Peter 1:16. Unless it can be clearly shown that the gospel "genre"
allowed for such "creative" activity on the part of authors, it must be
acknowledged that redaction criticism leaves the Evangelists guilty of
deception.

    2. Are we to believe that the Evangelists felt themselves free to
alter radically the message of Jesus and to "make up" events that never
happened during his ministry, even though there were eyewitnesses
still living who could easily point out their errors? We can believe that
only if no believers were concerned about the historical accuracy of the
Gospels, or none of the Gospels was written before all significant
eyewitnesses were dead. With regard to the interest in historical accuracy, remember what was mentioned contrary to this suggestion in the
previous paragraph. And with regard to the presence of eyewitnesses,
the redaction critics themselves have typically dated the Gospels fairly
early. For example, according to Marxsen, Mark was written in A.D.
66—long before the death of the last eyewitness of Jesus' ministry.

---

factor. . . . Christian scholars sometimes get near to accepting the view that some of
the New Testament writers were downright dishonest. . . . I believe that one is bound
to set over against the necessity to be alive to tendentiousness the fact that the
traditions about Jesus do reflect in him a new level of penetrating veracity, some of
which may be expected to have 'rubbed off' on his disciples and followers" ("The
Techniques of New Testament Research," in *Jesus and Man's Hope,* ed. Donald G.
Miller and Dikran Y. Hadidian [Pittsburgh: Pittsburgh Theological Seminary, 1971],
36–37).

    [82]Perrin, *What Is Redaction Criticism?* 73.
    [83]Ibid., 75.

Conclusion

THE CONSIDERATION OF THE POSITIONS advanced by Rudolf Bultmann (form criticism in particular) and by his immediate disciples (redaction criticism in particular) is a most fitting point at which to end this brief survey of the historical roots of Gospels criticism. It is now generally recognized that the Bultmannian period in New Testament criticism was of epochal significance, and that none of the various "new" approaches to the understanding of the Gospels proposed since then has achieved anything approaching the Bultmannian consensus in the mid-twentieth century.

Indeed, what seems most characteristic of biblical and theological studies today, in this concluding decade of the twentieth century, is the insistence that there is no single "true" understanding of the Gospels and of the Jesus whom they present. Edgar V. McKnight, for example, expresses the judgment that while many may view the vision of the new pluralism as "a nightmare," it is here to stay.

> It may be that we are, in the words of Dan Via, simply between the Bultmanns—that is, perhaps one world view will overwhelm us and a new "Bultmann," who has internalized that world view, will capture

151

our allegiance and bring a type of unity that does not now exist. I think not. Our community of biblical scholars will, in my opinion, cooperate in the future . . . by recognizing the inevitability and richness of diversity.[1]

The form-critical approach itself continues to be popular, if only as one of the many competing voices in Gospels study today. In our Introduction we referred to the "Jesus Seminar" and to its headline-grabbing method of voting on the authenticity of the various sayings attributed to Jesus in the Gospels. That seminar continues to meet annually and to employ its now somewhat old-fashioned form-critical criteria.[2]

But many new emphases have been put forward in the past quarter-century. In the 1970s, use of the analytical-critical methods of the social sciences became popular. Liberation (Latin American), black, and feminist theologians in particular introduced concepts originating from a Marxist matrix into Gospels studies, concepts such as the "hermeneutics of suspicion" and "interpreter praxis."[3] Research has continued into the social and religious world of first-century Judaism.[4] Some have concentrated on genre studies, comparing the canonical Gospels with the literary conventions of that time—with Greco-Roman

---

[1] Edgar V. McKnight, *Post-Modern Use of the Bible: The Emergence of Reader-oriented Criticism* (Nashville: Abingdon, 1988), 61. The reference to Via is to Dan O. Via, Jr., "A Quandary of Contemporary New Testament Scholarship: The Time Between the 'Bultmanns,'" *Journal of Religion* 55 (1975): 456–61.

[2] As this Conclusion is being written, the author's eye falls on this headline on page A-5 of the *San Diego Union-Tribune* for October 17, 1994: "Jesus Seminar scholars' verdict: Christ was not born of a virgin."

[3] Seminal works have been Gustavo Gutierrez, *A Theology of Liberation,* rev. ed. (Maryknoll, N.Y.: Orbis, 1988); James H. Cone, *A Black Theology of Liberation,* 2d ed. (Maryknoll, N.Y.: Orbis, 1986); and Elisabeth Schussler Fiorenza, *Bread Not Stone: The Challenge of Feminist Biblical Interpretation* (Boston: Beacon, 1986).

[4] See Gerd Theissen, *Sociology of Early Palestinian Christianity* (Philadelphia: Fortress, 1978). John Dominic Crossan is representative of recent attempts to make use of a variety of methodologies. In two books published in 1993 by Harper (*The Historical Jesus* and *Jesus: A Revolutionary Biography*) he concludes that Jesus of Nazareth was a peasant Jewish Cynic, a radical social revolutionary, a compassionate healer, and a proclaimer of "the unmediated presence of God" (*The Historical Jesus,* 423).

biography,[5] or with the ancient art of narrative (storytelling).[6] The advocates of canonical criticism have drawn attention to the ways in which the church has made use of the Scriptures after the completion of the canon, after that earliest history upon which source, form, and redaction criticism have concentrated.[7]

Many contemporary critics have moved the focus away from the historical Jesus (or the original believing community, or the Gospel writer) to today's readers and their "need for meaning that coheres with the reader's own situation in the world."[8] Structuralism, which just a short time ago was being hailed as a promising new direction in the literary study of the Gospels,[9] is now being described as merely an "interlude"[10] that has been superseded by deconstructionism, with its denial of the existence of any "deep structure" determining the meaning of the text, or indeed of any "real world" in terms of which the text must be understood, thus rejecting the notion that there is any "correct" interpretation of the text at all.[11]

McKnight insists that in all ages "readers have been reducing the text to their idiom, naturalizing the text so that it speaks to them."[12] What he sees as the fresh contribution of the "reader-oriented" view of

[5]Richard A. Burridge, *What Are the Gospels? A Comparison with Graeco-Roman Biography* (Cambridge: Cambridge University Press, 1992).

[6]See G. Theissen, *The Shadow of the Galilean: The Quest of the Historical Jesus in Narrative Form* (Philadelphia: Fortress, 1987).

[7]See Brevard S. Childs, *The New Testament as Canon: An Introduction* (Philadelphia: Fortress, 1984), and James A. Sanders, *Canon and Community: A Guide to Canonical Criticism* (Philadelphia: Fortress, 1984).

[8]McKnight, *Post-Modern Use of the Bible*, 107.

[9]See Daniel Patte, *What Is Structural Exegesis?* (Philadelphia: Fortress, 1976), and Vern Poythress, "Structuralism and Biblical Studies," *Journal of the Evangelical Theological Society* 21:3 (September 1978): 221–38.

[10]E. V. McKnight, "Literary Criticism," in *Dictionary of Jesus and the Gospels*, eds. Joel B. Green and Scot McKnight (Downers Grove, Illinois: InterVarsity Press, 1992), 478.

[11]See especially Jacques Derrida, *Of Grammatology,* trans. Gayatri Chakravorty Spivak (Baltimore: John Hopkins University Press, 1976), and Mark C. Taylor, *Erring: A Postmodern A/Theology* (Chicago: University of Chicago Press, 1984). For helpful introductory descriptions, see the articles on "Deconstructionism," "Postmodern Theology," and "Structuralism" in *A New Handbook of Christian Theology*, eds. Donald W. Musser and Joseph L. Price (Nashville: Abingdon, 1992).

[12]McKnight, *Post-Modern Use of the Bible,* 150.

the Bible is (1) the recognition that this engagement of the "creative imaginations"[13] of the readers, so that "readers *make* sense"[14] of the text, is the proper use of all literature (including the Bible) and (2) the recognition that the distinctive characteristic and "challenge" of our "post-modern" world is that "our world view does not dictate one perspective and approach."[15] "Today pluralism reigns."[16]

The ongoing history of Gospels criticism, therefore, can be seen as the ongoing history of attempts to bring the gospel witness into harmony with the prevailing philosophical and cultural moods of the age. Intellectual honesty forces some contemporary scholars to an outright repudiation of Jesus, his message and movement. Many others continue to be attracted to the Gospels by ties of affection or ecclesiastical tradition and continue to seek some legitimization linking their own worldview with the Jesus presented in the Gospels.

The way commanded to us in the Bible itself, however, remains the same today as yesterday: to seek to bring our every thought captive to the obedience of Christ (2 Cor. 10:5). Not the Christ remade in our own image, shaped by our shifting contemporary standards of the true and the valuable, but the Christ presented to us in the "God-breathed" Scriptures (2 Tim. 3:16), God's written Word and our only ultimate authority for faith and life.[17]

---

[13]Ibid., 105.

[14]Ibid., 161.

[15]Ibid., 150–51.

[16]Ibid., 152.

[17]A helpful analysis of the fact that the predominant views of history that have controlled modern biblical criticism are fundamentally out of accord with the view presented in the Bible itself is presented in Ned B. Stonehouse, *Origins of the Synoptic Gospels: Some Basic Questions* (Grand Rapids: Eerdmans, 1963), 176–92. As Stonehouse writes: "Only if the witness of the Gospels to Jesus and that of Jesus' self-revelation are taken at face value . . . will one be able to establish genuine continuity between Jesus and the Gospel tradition. . . . Only if he is the divine Messiah, can we understand the history in which those who from the beginning were eyewitnesses and ministers of the Word, acting with his authority, delivered over to the Church a knowledge of the Gospel tradition. And this history is intelligible also only as we grasp the fact that the divine Messiah, who was endowed with the Spirit of God in a unique fashion, himself qualified his spokesmen and representatives with an enduement of the Spirit from on high that they might bear witness to him."

Index of Persons

Index of Scripture